Making Library Web Sites Usable

A LITA Guide

Tom Lehman

and Terry Nikkel

LIBRARY AND INFORMATION TECHNOLOGY ASSOCIATION

Neal-Schuman Publishers, Inc.
New York   London

Published by Neal-Schuman Publishers, Inc.
100 William St., Suite 2004
New York, NY 10038

Printed and bound in the United States of America.

The paper used in this publication meets the minimum requirements of American National Standard for Information Sciences - Permanence of Paper for Printed Library Materials, ANSI Z39.48-1992.

Library of Congress Cataloging-in-Publication Data

Lehman, Tom, 1947-
    Making library Web sites usable : a LITA guide / Tom Lehman, Terry Nikkel.
        p. cm. — (LITA guides ; no. 14)
    Includes bibliographical references and index.
    ISBN 978-1-55570-620-3 (alk. paper)
1. Library Web sites—Design. 2. Library Web sites—United States—Case studies.
I. Nikkel, Terry. II. Title.
Z674.75.W67L44 2008
006.701'9—dc22
                                                        2008043245

Table of Contents

v

vii

List of Figures

Preface

Libraries no longer have a near-monopoly on providing information. A fairly recent OCLC (2005) study found that 89 percent of college students begin their research on the Internet, while only 2 percent start in library catalogs. Library Web sites contain a wealth of resources and services but, for many users, suffer from usability issues in comparison to search engines. Difficult-to-learn syntax, unintuitive index terms, and poor relevance ranking often leave users confused. Anyone who has watched a first-year student struggle to find articles for a paper on a library Web site can attest to this.

Having a friendly, usable, attractive site is now a base expectation. For impatient users who consider themselves tech savvy, one difficult experience can be enough to send them off to Google, Yahoo!, or another more intuitive information gateway. If their Web sites perplex patrons, libraries risk becoming marginalized.

Through their Web sites, libraries can now provide service to individuals both in their own communities and across the world. Researchers can find out more easily about specialized collections, and full-text collections and databases enable access for both regular customers who are traveling and remote researchers. A user-friendly Web site allows the library to take full advantage of the Internet.

Libraries face some significant challenges in creating usable Web sites, making usability testing even more important. Integrating resources hosted in disparate databases and providing quick and easy access to a diverse and ever-growing range of online information is a formidable task. Most libraries must provide both information and services on the same Web site, something that many other organizations do not yet do. Libraries are also notorious for employing jargon that others don't understand. Usability testing helps site developers understand and identify these and other challenges so they can be dealt with before customers ever encounter them.

Making Library Web Sites Usable is part of the LITA Guides series. Like other books in the series, it combines LITA's ongoing interest in, and promotion of, usability testing with its reputation for expert-authored books that make technical topics accessible to a wide range of information professionals. The contributors all have practical experience in usability and offer advice based on their successes and failures. They have worked as Webmasters, members of Web teams, and administrators; they also come from academic, corporate, and public library backgrounds, thus offering a broad overview of applications and perspectives.

The chapters of *Making Library Web Sites Usable* examine each step of the usability process, including the formation of a project team, selecting a technique or techniques, attracting subjects, conducting the test in an effective and unbiased way, and applying the results to address problems uncovered in the original site or mockup.

Making Library Web Sites Usable covers the most common usability methods, as well as exploring some of the difficulties of usability testing. The goal is to provide solid grounding for beginners, as well as introduce those with some background in the area to new techniques and ways of refining their skills. Even experienced readers may not be aware of all the ways in which methods can be combined or how techniques more commonly used in businesses can apply to libraries.

Effective usability programs are well designed, supported by administration, communicated to stakeholders within the library, coordinated by a dedicated team, and are ongoing rather than one-time projects. They incorporate more than one usability technique, applying these techniques to the whole site, not just the home page. Testers select subjects to reflect the primary sectors of the library's user community. In *Making Library Web Sites Usable*, we strive to show how this ideal can be possible for all institutions.

Organization

Chapter 1, "Usability for Library Web Sites," introduces usability assessment and its application to libraries. Chapters 2–8 discuss the primary assessment techniques: Heuristic evaluations, surveys, focus group interviews, card sorting, paper prototyping, usability testing, and log analysis.

The next three chapters tackle general issues in testing. Chapter 9, "Attracting Users for Testing," addresses techniques for finding willing participants. Chapter 10, "Low-Cost Usability Recording," explores the strategic use of economical software. Chapter 11, "Communicating Usability Results Effectively," shows readers how best to disseminate their data to the entire library staff and increase support for Web site changes.

Chapters 12–17 present assessment in action. Academic libraries serve as models in three of these chapters, with one each from a public library, corporate library, and a government or special library. Chapter 12 reports on a test at Purdue University, which led to a major redesign. This case study highlights many elements of an ideal, or classic, usability assessment. Chapter 13 portrays University of Virginia, a library with a commitment to iterative, standards-based testing of all new and updated Web sites. Chapter 14 describes user testing done at Wright State University to gather reactions and input on a proposed new service.

Chapter 15 depicts usability testing at a rapidly growing public library system. Chapter 16 discusses a multi-stage program at a large, distributed corporate library, focusing on the challenges of providing access to both internal and external content in a single interface. Finally, Chapter 17 covers usability testing done at NASA's Goddard Library under the constraint of needing to adopt new systemwide Web page templates.

The bibliography section presents a number of selected resources for those wishing to dig deeper. For each topic, the editors sought to identify two to four journal articles on the tool, one or two Web sites devoted to information on the topic, and one or two of the most important books, if available. The annotations provide brief descriptions to assist in identifying resources that match the readers' needs.

We hope readers will come away from *Making Library Web Sites Usable* convinced of the importance of usability, with an understanding of how best to undertake each type of testing and how to combine a variety of methods effectively. Intelligent planning through usability testing helps libraries ensure that their invaluable information sources remain accessible in the Internet age.

Reference

OCLC. 2005. "Perceptions of Libraries and Information Resources." Available: www.oclc.org/reports/2005perceptions.htm

Acknowledgments

This book has its origins in the *MyLibrary Manual*, conceived and organized by Eric Lease Morgan as a resource with two goals: to provide information and guidance for implementers of the MyLibrary software he developed at North Carolina State University beginning in 1997; and to articulate and promote the principals of user-centered design for digital libraries. Terry Nikkel, author of one of the *MyLibrary Manual* chapters and a member of the LITA Publications Committee, proposed that the usability chapters of the Manual be used as the basis for a book on library Web site usability, to serve as a revision of the 2001 LITA guide on library Web site usability. This book would not have come about without both their contributions, or without the chapter authors who generously contributed their time and expertise. The book's strengths are theirs—any weaknesses, the editors'.

Usability for Library Web Sites

Tom Lehman and Terry Nikkel

Introduction

When the Internet revolution took off in the early 1990s, libraries faced a major challenge: What they should collect and how they should provide access to collections and services in the new electronic environment. In the last 10 years, most libraries have incorporated the Web into the way they do business. For most academic library users, and increasingly for public and special library users, the library Web site is the primary gateway to vast information holdings, allowing users to learn about, navigate, search, and obtain library resources and services without ever entering a library building. This transformation has brought many benefits; however, it also has created problems. Libraries, which once had a near-monopoly as information providers, face increasing competition from online information providers who, unhampered by constraints faced by libraries, are able to take advantage of the capabilities of the new medium to provide easy and quick access to information. Many users, particularly younger ones, have responded by making the Internet the first source for their information needs and the library among the last, frequently consulting a library Web site only when the information need is great and other alternatives have not been successful. An OCLC survey found that 89 percent of college students began their research on the Internet, while only 2 percent started in library catalogs (2006). It is ironic that, as libraries have recognized and responded to the need to provide more of their collections and services online, users have been abandoning them for other information providers such as Google and Yahoo!

Although many reasons can be cited for this, the difficulty users have using many library Web sites, in comparison with other online information sources, is by far the most important. Jakob Nielsen, a well-known Web site usability expert, states, "If a Web site is difficult to use, people leave. . . . If users get lost on a Web site, they leave. If a Web site's information is hard to read or doesn't answer users' key questions, they leave" (2003: n.p.). If potential library users continue to use non-library information sources and ignore library Web sites, libraries risk being marginalized. Libraries have a significant interest in making their Web sites easier to use and more attuned to the way users have become accustomed to searching for and using information. This book shows how to make library Web sites more usable.

What Is Usability?

Nielsen defines usability as "[A] quality attribute assessing how easy user interfaces are to use" (2003: n.p.). Another frequently cited definition of usability appears in ISO standard 9241-11, which defines it as "The extent to which a product can be used by specified users to achieve specified goals with effectiveness, efficiency and satisfaction in a specified context of use" (ISO, 1998).

Nielsen goes on, "The word 'usability' also refers to methods for improving ease-of-use during the design process" (2003: n.p.). Here are some additional related usability concepts that are described and used in this book: "Usability methods" refers to specific techniques to determine how easy or difficult a Web site is to use. "Usability assessment" is used to describe the process of using one or more usability methods to determine the level of usability of a Web site. Finally, "usability program" refers to the entire process of designing and conducting a usability assessment, analyzing the results and identifying key findings, determining changes that are needed in the Web site, creating one or more possible solutions, testing the solutions, implementing the preferred solution, and then starting the process all over again.

At heart, usability methods and processes are ways of focusing on users to meet their needs and preferred ways of finding and using information, and to involve them in the Web site design process. Libraries that know, understand, and involve users in the Web assessment and design process will create Web sites that succeed in meeting users' needs and expectations.

Usability in Libraries

While library Web sites share many characteristics with other Web sites, in some important respects libraries suffer significant disadvantages that make their Web sites harder to make usable. Here are the most critical:

1. Unlike most commercial sites, libraries don't actually own the information being provided online. Amazon, Best Buy, and others can provide a single search across the whole range of items they sell, whereas libraries typically provide access to dozens or hundreds of databases from different vendors, usually with their own proprietary search interface, distinct search techniques, and syntax. Many users lack the

patience to learn the peculiarities of each and are understandably attracted to one-box-search-everything types of sites.

2. The venerable library catalog, formerly the premier library information source, suffers badly in comparison with its new online competitors. Users find the catalog hard to use, with its arcane search techniques, unintuitive subject headings, and relevance ranking that is rudimentary or nonexistent. Users, accustomed to seeing desired information in the top three results of a Google search, are likely to go elsewhere when confronted with library catalog search results sets consisting of hundreds or thousands of records in no discernable order. Attempts are being made to address these problems: The Endeca catalog at North Carolina State University (www.lib.ncsu.edu/catalog/), the Primo service being developed by Ex Libris (www.exlibrisgroup.com), and the Extensible Catalog being developed at University of Rochester with funding from the Mellon Foundation (http://extensiblecatalog.info) are steps in the right direction.

3. Library Web sites typically begin as Web pages created by librarians, with organization and terminology that make sense to librarians rather than to users. To a large extent, this continues to be the case in library Web sites that do not follow a systematic approach to usability.

4. Finally, libraries typically lack the technical expertise to stay abreast of and implement the rapidly advancing Web 2.0 technologies to which users are becoming accustomed: RSS, AJAX, auto-suggest, social tagging, and so on.

There is no single solution that will fix all these challenges, but an indispensable component of libraries' strategies to address them is to create usability programs that are well designed, supported at top levels of library administration, well communicated and understood by stakeholders within the library, and are ongoing rather than one-time projects.

Building Effective Library Usability Programs

Some characteristics of effective library usability programs include:

1. Getting started. Applying usability methods described in subsequent chapters will return benefits at any level of application, from the simple, task-based usability testing performed by a novice to the systematic, iterative usability assessment carried out by library staff with extensive usability experience. The key is to get started and keep learning.

2. Cultivation of usability expertise at both the individual and group level. An important first step forward might be to designate an individual to take responsibility for learning about usability to lead the usability

program, whether full- or part-time. Library usability programs will be most effective when usability expertise is dispersed throughout the library. Where feasible, a group should be assigned responsibility for the library usability program.

3. Combining theory and practice. Experience and professional reading and involvement are equally valuable and complement each other.

Suggestions for Usability Beginners

For those getting started with usability:

1. Begin with task-based usability testing and seek to master it, but over time learn and use all the usability methods. Each has its strengths and weaknesses. Applying usability methods in combination allows them to complement each other and give more complete and reliable information than using just one. For example:

   a) *Focus group interviews and surveys*
      These two methods work well together: Focus group interviews allow in-depth probing and analysis, while surveys allow systematic polling of larger numbers of users, providing quantitative data that can be used to determine the extent to which a problem or opinion is shared among the user population as a whole.

   b) *Card sorting and paper prototyping*
      This combination of methods can be used to identify issues with terminology and Web site organization. Paper prototype testing can identify problems with existing terminology ("What would you expect to see if you clicked this link?"), while card sorting can give insights into how users would group resources so they make sense to them, and terms that make sense to describe the groupings.

   c) *Log analysis and surveys*
      Surveys can be used to determine how important users think individual library resources are to them, while log analysis makes it possible to track the actual usage of the resources. This can be useful information to have when trying to redesign a too-crowded Web page.

   d) *Usability testing with interviews or surveys*
      Usability testing makes it possible to see what users actually do. Usability tests— particularly tests that compare two different interfaces—can be usefully followed up with interviews or surveys of test participants ("Which interface was easier to use and why?" or "On a scale of 1–5, rank each Web site on the following characteristics.").

2. Expand the scope of usability assessment. Do not limit the application of usability methods to the library home page, although that's a

good place to start. Other appropriate applications of usability methods include:

a) Testing proposed services, as described by Annam and Aldrich in the Wright State University case study (Chapter 14).

b) Testing features of the Web site. Two examples from usability testing done at the University of Notre Dame:

   (1) Usability testing done to improve the design of a "Contact the Libraries" page.

   (2) A post-implementation survey carried out to gather information on the level of use and acceptance of a new "Find articles" (meta-search) page.

c) Use beyond the Web site to build the library's usability expertise and user focus. Two more examples from the University of Notre Dame:

   (1) Focus group interviews conducted to determine how graduate students prefer to get information about new library resources and services.

   (2) Usability testing conducted to determine how to improve the wording of the link text URLs in records for electronic serial records in the catalog.

Potential Pitfalls

Several aspects of usability programs commonly cause some problems for new practitioners, but awareness of them and their solutions will minimize their impact.

5

First, it is important to be clear on why the usability testing is being done and what information is needed to move forward. Considerable frustration can result from usability tests that do not return the needed information, where test participants are not behaving as expected, resulting in wasted effort. Pretesting the usability test with representative members of the user population is the most important way to prevent wasted tests. Another is performing careful analysis and planning at the beginning.

Second, as a library begins usability testing for the first time, staff can become very enthused by the valuable insights being gained and tempted to implement the "obvious" solution immediately. As they gain experience though, the importance of recording and documenting results will become apparent. Testing becomes more valuable as it is repeated. Having a record of prior usability testing, the questions asked, and raw and summarized results will be invaluable.

Third, the "obvious" solution to a problem sometimes actually is not, so the issue of how to interpret test results becomes very important. In one all-too-common example, the user found the page with the answer to the question but did not see it and gave up or looked elsewhere. Was the reason that:

- the font was too small?
- the text was overwhelmed by graphics?
- the page was too busy?
- the terminology did not match the user's vocabulary?

Several things can be done to help interpret test results properly and improve the likelihood of finding design solutions that address the specific problems testing uncovered, including:

1. Debrief users after tests. "In task 4, why did you click on link X?"
2. Don't jump to a conclusion. Consider alternative explanations of the observed behavior.
3. Create and test alternative explanations by designing quick mockups to see if any are easier for users.

(Jared Spool has a good discussion of interpreting test results at http://www. uie.com/events/roadshow/articles/recommendation/)

Finally, communication about usability assessment has to involve all library staff, not just Web site stakeholders. Covered in detail in Chapter 11, this is an important step in obtaining buy-in and involvement and in avoiding the need to defend procedures and conclusions later on.

Conclusion

While usability may not make your library Web site as easy to use or as popular as Google, an effective usability program will make users' needs more likely to be met, and the library's Web site more likely to be used. Libraries are facing unprecedented challenges—and opportunities—from the changes taking place on the Internet. Business-as-usual is not an effective option in the long run. Libraries and librarians who focus on users, seeking them out to learn about their needs and involving them not only in testing at the end of the process but from the beginning in Web site design, will make their Web sites usable.

References

ISO (1998)9241-11:1998. 1998. *Ergonomic Requirements for Office Work with Video Display Terminals, Part 11: Guidance on Usability*. Geneva, Switzerland: International Organization for Standardization.

Nielsen, Jakob. 2003. "Usability 101: Introduction to Usability" (August 25). Available: www.useit.com/alertbox/20030825.html (accessed June 18, 2007).

OCLC. 2006. "College Students' Perceptions of Libraries and Information Resources. Part 1: Libraries and Information Resources—Use, Familiarity and Favorability." Available: www.oclc.org/reports/pdfs/studentperceptions_part1.pdf (accessed June 18, 2007).

Chapter 2

Heuristics

Hal P. Kirkwood, Jr.

Heuristic evaluation is a usability engineering method for finding the usability problems in a user interface design so that they can be attended to as part of an iterative design process. Heuristic evaluation involves having a small set of evaluators examine the interface and judge its compliance with recognized usability principles (the "heuristics")

(Nielsen, 2005a: n.p.)

Introduction

Heuristic evaluations are an analytical method of site testing rather than true usability testing. They should be considered one part of an assessment or design plan that should also include usability testing. By conducting heuristic evaluations prior to usability testing, common problems within the site can be identified and corrected prior to testing with users.

Types of Heuristics

Jakob Nielsen's original usability heuristics consist of 10 principles for user interface design. The heuristics were developed to serve as broad principles or guidelines for assessing an interface's usability. Covering a variety of general user expectations when using an application or visiting a Web site, the heuristics are the foundation for analyzing user interaction with a site. Modification of the heuristics is often useful and necessary, depending on a site's purpose and functions.

Jakob Nielsen's Heuristics (Nielsen, 2005b)

1. *Visibility of system status*

    The system should always keep users informed about what is going on, through appropriate feedback within reasonable time.

2. *Match between system and the real world*

    The system should speak the users' language, with words, phrases, and concepts familiar to the user, rather than system-oriented terms. Follow

7

real-world conventions, making information appear in a natural and logical order.

3. *User control and freedom*

Users often choose system functions by mistake and will need a clearly marked "emergency exit" to leave the unwanted state without having to go through an extended dialogue. Support undo and redo.

4. *Consistency and standards*

Users should not have to wonder whether different words, situations, or actions mean the same thing. Follow platform conventions.

5. *Error prevention*

Even better than good error messages is a careful design that prevents a problem from occurring in the first place. Either eliminate error-prone conditions or check for them and present users with a confirmation option before they commit to the action.

6. *Recognition rather than recall*

Minimize the user's memory load by making objects, actions, and options visible. The user should not have to remember information from one part of the dialogue to another. Instructions for use of the system should be visible or easily retrievable whenever appropriate.

7. *Flexibility and efficiency of use*

Accelerators—unseen by the novice user—may often speed up the interaction for the expert user such that the system can cater to both inexperienced and experienced users. Allow users to tailor frequent actions.

8. *Aesthetic and minimalist design*

Dialogues should not contain information that is irrelevant or rarely needed. Every extra unit of information in a dialogue competes with the relevant units of information and diminishes their relative visibility.

9. *Help users recognize, diagnose, and recover from errors*

Error messages should be expressed in plain language (no codes), precisely indicate the problem, and constructively suggest a solution.

10. *Help and documentation*

Even though it is better if the system can be used without documentation, it may be necessary to provide help and documentation. Any such information should be easy to search, focused on the user's task, list concrete steps to be carried out, and not be too large.

The Web Usability Team at the University of Virginia adapted Nielsen's heuristics to fit library site design. They separated the heuristics into three logically grouped categories.

University of Virginia Web Usability Team Heuristics (University of Virginia, 2003)

Information Structure and Navigation

1. *Intelligible information structure*
   Interface organizes and presents information in easily understood and easily accessible manner; initial levels of information should be concise, easy to scan, allowing progressive access to more extensive info.
   [*cf.* Error prevention; User control; Flexibility & efficiency]

2. *Use of plain language*
   Interface avoids jargon, organizes information according to user expectations rather than organization insiders.
   [*cf.* Match w/ real world]

3. *Intuitive, efficient and flexible navigation*
   User can get back to home page, move up and down the information hierarchy easily (i.e., get back to the top of subsection, switch to other branch of the information tree).
   [*cf.* User control; Flexibility & efficiency]

4. *Orientation*
   Intuitive visual cues to orient the visitor to a location within the site (e.g., breadcrumbs, page headers, etc.).
   [*cf.* Visibility of system status]

Content and Design

5. *Consistent placement of interface elements*
   Primary and secondary navigation, help, search, contact, other supporting information (e.g., menus, footer, banner).
   [*cf.* Consistency & standards; Recognition; Help]

6. *Consistent use of language and labeling in interface*
   Stylistic consistency in spelling, capitalization, etc. (e.g., "Questions?" button to send e-mail to a librarian; VIRGO Search form; "e-mail" always hyphenated).
   [*cf.* Recognition vs. recall; Consistency & standards; Recognition; Help and documentation; Match w/ real world]

7. *Consistent, effective and appropriate design*
   Consistency with site-wide design standards (logo, basic layout, color palette, etc.); effective presentation of information; appropriate use of graphics (including use of ALT tags); consistent typography; appropriate and efficient image compression for optimal download time; avoidance of gratuitous icons, unnecessary graphics.
   [*cf.* Aesthetics & minimalist design]

9

Specific to Search Forms and Data Manipulation

8. *Error prevention*

    Clear indications regarding restricted-access resources; select menus instead of text input).

    [*cf.* Error prevention]

9. *Supports expert users*

    Accelerators, shortcuts, search options; saving and reviewing results and parameters.

    [*cf.* Flexibility and efficiency of use; User control]

10. *Useful error reports*

    Informative, plain language error messages; uniformity of language in error messages; system suggests search strategies.

    [cf. Error recovery] (University of Virginia, 2003).

The Web Site Support Team at Purdue University developed a set of heuristics based on Nielsen's Heuristics and Lazarski's Web Heuristics form, developed for a college Web design course. The team's heuristics consisted of the following seven sections; the specific questions are listed to provide detail into what was being checked by evaluators. These are the types of specific questions that need to be developed and then answered during heuristic evaluations.

Purdue University Web Site Support Team Heuristics

(The following heuristics were developed by the Heuristic Sub-team of the Web Site Support Team, Purdue University Libraries, Jan Addison and Katie Clark, and are reproduced with permission by the original authors.)

1. *Clarity of Communication:* Tests the overall clear sense of audience for the Website, the use of language, and presentation of information in an orderly fashion.

    a) Does the site/page convey a clear sense of its intended audience (student, faculty, etc.)?

    b) Does it use language in a way that is familiar to and comfortable for its readers?

    c) Does it present information in a logical and natural order?

    d) Is the user interface efficient, allowing fast orientation and good results by experienced users?

    e) Is the user interface easy to remember? Imagine you are a user who is going to use the site infrequently.

2. *Accessibility:* Tests for load time, accessibility for disadvantaged readers, user tailorability, and ease of learning the system.

    a) Is load time appropriate to content, even on a slow dial-up connection?

    b) Is it accessible to readers with physical impairments? (e.g., is the text resizable and still intelligible?)

    c) Is the information accurate, complete, and understandable?

    d) Is there an easily discoverable means of communicating with the author or administrator?

    e) Does it accommodate a range of diverse user goals?

    f) Is there user tailorability to speed up frequent actions?

    g) Are there minimal graphics? (a consideration for fast loading)

    h) Is the site easy to learn?

3. *Consistency:* Tests for whether the site has a consistent, recognizable look and feel. Overall, this category indicates the site is in good shape.

    a) Does the site/page have a consistent, clearly recognizable "look-and-feel"?

    b) Does it make effective use of repeating visual themes to unify?

    c) Is it visually consistent even without graphics?

    d) Does it adhere to consistent conventions for layout, formatting, typefaces, labeling, etc.?

    e) Are icons labeled?

    f) Are there no more than 12 to 20 icon types?

    g) Are attention-getting techniques used with care? (e.g., used only for exceptional conditions or for time-dependent information?)

4. *Navigation:* Tests for standards in linking, link colors, and, in general, clear and consistent navigation.

    a) Does the site use standard link colors?

    b) Are the links obvious in their intent and destination?

    c) Is there a convenient, obvious way to maneuver among related pages and between different sections?

    d) Does the site make it easy to return to an initial state?

    e) Does the navigation allow the users to determine their position in the structure?

    f) Is there clear and consistent navigation?

    g) Forgiveness: Actions are reversible. Not locked into a page. If filling out a form, able to "clear".

    h) Does the "back" button work?

    i) Is the site searchable?

    j) Is the URL for the page easy to recall?

5. *Flexibility and Minimalist Design:* Tests for design elements that are effective yet minimal.

    a) Does the site/page make effective use of hyperlinks to tie related items together?

11

b) Are there dead links? Broken CGI or Java scripts? Functionless forms? Is it error-free?

c) Is page length appropriate to site content?

d) Are all icons in a set visually and conceptually distinct?

e) Are menu titles brief, yet long enough to communicate? (There should be a brief title of the page that appears at the top of the screen, too!)

f) Are there pop-up or pull-down menus within data entry fields that have many, but well defined, entry options?

g) Are the pages visually uncluttered?

h) Is there excessive use of Java scripts?

6. *Visual Presentation:* Tests for presentation elements that enhance rather than detract from the overall visual presentation.

a) Is the site moderate in its use of color?

b) Does it avoid juxtaposing text and animations?

c) Does it provide feedback whenever possible? (For example, through the use of an easily recognizable ALINK color or a "reply" screen for forms-based pages.)

d) Does it avoid blinking text or banner type logos?

e) Does the page appear reasonably similar when viewed via Netscape or Internet Explorer?

f) Are there underlined text phrases that are not hotlinks?

g) Is it easy to tell what is hotlinked on a page and what is not?

h) Is the user interface of the library site aesthetically well-designed— do you like it?

7. *Recognition Rather than Recall:* Tests for logical groupings of items into zones that indicate recognition rather than recall.

a) Have prompts been formatted using white space, justification, and visual cues for easy scanning?

b) Do text areas have "breathing space" around them?

c) Have items been grouped into logical zones, and have headings been used to distinguish between zones?

d) Have zones been separated by spaces, lines, color, letters, bold titles, rules lines, or shaded areas?

A crucial factor to remember when using or developing a set of heuristics is that they are flexible guidelines, not specific rules. The needs of users and the functions of a site can dictate design elements that contradict the heuristics.

Heuristic Evaluation

Basic heuristic evaluation begins with adopting or developing a set of heuristics to use as the foundation of the evaluation. The goal is to identify common problems within the site design. Evaluators compare the site to the specific elements of the heuristic. It is possible for one person to conduct a heuristic evaluation, but according to Nielsen (2005a), a small group of evaluators can identify a greater number of problems while only minimally increasing the cost of carrying out the evaluation. The evaluation is conducted on the Web site or a prototype, since heuristic evaluation does not require a functioning design. Using the heuristics, evaluators work to identify potential design problems. A useful practice is to compare and collate the results after the evaluators have completed their individual assessment. The heuristic evaluation will not provide solutions for the problems identified. Site designers will need to use Web design and information architecture principles to determine effective methods of fixing the problems.

A heuristic evaluation normally includes the following steps:

1. Develop or select an appropriate set of heuristics that matches the site's purpose.
2. Select 2–10 evaluators. Evaluators can be members of the design team or design-savvy members of the organization.
3. Explain the heuristics and provide the necessary evaluation forms (see Appendix 2A) to the evaluators.
4. Conduct the heuristic evaluation.
5. Collect each evaluator's list of problems and collate the results to develop a combined listing of the issues and problems.
6. Convey the results to the site's designers, who determine what changes are needed in the information architecture and design of the site to correct the problems identified.

Severity Ratings

An additional layer of heuristic evaluation can include severity ratings. According to Nielsen, the severity of the problems can be measured based on the "frequency, impact and persistence" of each problem ("Severity Ratings for Usability Problems," n.d.). The value of using severity ratings is to prioritize the problems for better efficiency in fixing them. Evaluators should assign severity ratings either individually or as a group using the combined list of problems. In spite of the fact that severity ratings may vary among evaluators, they can provide useful information to the site's designers.

Competitive/Comparative Heuristic Evaluation

Competitive/comparative evaluation can be a useful way for heuristic evaluators to develop a deeper understanding of common design elements implemented on similar sites. The evaluators use a common set of heuristics and evaluate a selection of similar sites. Patterns and common design elements may

13

be identified during the comparative evaluation. The repeated use of the heuristics develops a depth of familiarity that can be beneficial in future heuristic evaluations. Conducting a competitive/comparative evaluation prior to the heuristic evaluation of the site being redesigned can give evaluators experience with the process. By discussing their findings, evaluators can determine if there are variations in how they understand and apply the heuristic guidelines.

Library Web sites are particularly well suited for competitive/comparative heuristic evaluations because of the many common elements they contain, such as library catalogs, access to databases, instructional pages, and standard library services, to name only a few. Evaluators can develop an understanding of how other sites with similar purposes and resources have handled particular design issues. Finally, this type of evaluation can identify potential sites for use in benchmark comparisons.

Conclusion

Heuristic evaluation is the use of a set of guidelines to identify common usability issues or problems. It is one phase in an overall design plan, and should be supplemented with usability testing. In addition to heuristic evaluation, iterative redesign, prototyping, and usability testing will be needed to achieve a successful Web site redesign. Heuristic evaluation serves as an affordable method of identifying common and obvious problems before formal usability testing begins.

References

Nielsen, Jakob. 2005a. "How to Conduct a Heuristic Evaluation." Available: www.useit.com/papers/heuristic/heuristic_evaluation.html

————. 2005b. "Ten Usability Heuristics." Available: www.useit.com/papers/heuristic/heuristic_list.html

————. n.d. "Severity Ratings for Usability Problems." Available: www.useit.com/papers/heuristic/severityrating.html

University of Virginia Web Usability Team. 2003. Web Usability Testing, University of Virginia Library. Available: www.lib.virginia.edu/usability/index.html

Appendix 2A: Heuristic Evaluation Form

Scoring:
0 = Not applicable; 1 = No problem; 2 = Minor or slight problem;
3 = Major problem

1. Clarity of communication

This category tests the overall clear sense of audience for the Website, the use of language, and presentation of information in an orderly fashion.

	Average over all pages
1a. Does the site/page convey a clear sense of its intended audience?	
1b. Does it use language in a way that is familiar to and comfortable for its readers?	
1d. Does it present information in a logical and natural order?	
1e. Is the user interface efficient, allowing fast orientation and good results by an experienced user?	
1f. Is the user interface easy to remember? Imagine you are a user who is going to use the site infrequently.	

2. Accessibility

This category tests for load time, accessibility for disadvantaged readers, user tailorability, and ease of learning the system.

	Average over all pages
2a. Is load time appropriate to content, even on a slow dial-up connection?	
2b. Is it accessible to readers with physical impairments? In other words, is the text resizable and still intelligible?	
2c. Is the information accurate, complete, and understandable?	
2d. Is there an easily discoverable means of communicating with the author or administrator?	
2e. Does it accommodate a range of diverse user goals?	
2f. Is there user tailorability to speed up frequent actions?	

(Cont'd.)

15

Appendix 2A: Heuristic Evaluation Form *(Continued)*

2. Accessibility *(Cont'd.)*

	Average over all pages
2g. Are there mininal graphics? (A consideration for fast loading.)	
2h. Is the system easy to learn?	

3. Consistency

This category tests for whether the site has a consistent, recognizable look and feel.

	Average over all pages
3a. Does the site/page have a consistent, clearly recognizable look and feel?	
3b. Does it make effective use of repeating visual themes to unify?	
3c. Is it visually consistent even without graphics?	
3d. Does it adhere to consistent conventions for layout, formatting, typefaces, labeling etc.?	
3e. Are icons labeled?	
3f. Are there no more than 12 to 20 icon types?	
3g. Are attention-getting techniques used with care? (e.g., used only for exceptional conditions or for time-dependent information)	

4. Navigation

This category tests for standards in linking, link colors, and, in general, clear and consistent navigation.

	Average over all pages
4a. Does the site use standard link colors?	
4b. Are the links obvious in their intent and destination?	
4c. Is there a convenient, obvious way to maneuver among related pages and between different sections?	
	(Cont'd.)

16

Appendix 2A: Heuristic Evaluation Form *(Continued)*

4. Navigation *(Cont'd.)*

	Average over all pages
4d. Does the site make it easy to return to an initial state?	
4e. Does the navigation allow the users to determine their position in the structure?	
4f. Is there clear and consistent navigation?	
4g. Forgiveness: Actions are reversible. Not locked into a page. If filling out a form, able to "clear".	
4h. Does the "back" button work?	
4i. Is the site searchable?	
4j. Is the URL for the page easy to recall?	

5. Flexibility and minimalist design
This category tests for design elements that are effective yet minimal.

	Average over all pages
5a. Does the site/page make effective use of hyperlinks to tie related items together?	
5b. Are there dead links? Broken CGI or Java scripts? Functionless forms? Is it error-free?	
5c. Is page length appropriate to site content?	
5d. Are all icons in a set visually and conceptually distinct?	
5e. Are menu titles brief, yet long enough to communicate? (There should be a brief title of the page that appears at the top of the screen, too!)	
5f. Are there pop-up or pull-down menus within data entry fields that have many, but well defined entry options?	
5g. Are the pages visually uncluttered?	
5h. Is there excessive use of Java scripts?	

(Cont'd.)

17

Appendix 2A: Heuristic Evaluation Form *(Continued)*

6. Visual presentation

This category tests for presentation elements that enhance rather than detract from the overall visual presentation.

	Average over all pages
6a. Is the site moderate in its use of color?	
6b. Does it avoid juxtaposing text and animations?	
6c. Does it provide feedback whenever possible? (For example, through the use of an easily recognizable ALINK color or a "reply" screen for forms-based pages)	
6d. Does it avoid blinking text or banner type logos?	
6e. Does the page appear reasonably similar when viewed via Netscape or Internet Explorer?	
6f. Are there underlined text phrases that are not hotlinks?	
6g. Is it easy to tell what is hotlinked on a page and what is not?	
6h. Is the user interface of THOR aesthetically well designed— do you like it?	

7. Recognition rather than recall

This category tests for logical groupings of items into zones that indicate recognition rather than recall.

	Average over all pages
7a. Have prompts been formatted using white space, justification, and visual cues for easy scanning?	
7b. Do text areas have "breathing space" around them?	
7c. Have items been grouped into logical zones, and have headings been used to distinguish between zones?	
7d. Have zones been separated by spaces, lines, color, letters, bold titles, rules lines, or shaded areas?	

Chapter 3

Surveys
Tom Lehman

Introduction

Surveys— sometimes called questionnaires—are a method of gathering information about the perceptions, habits, attitudes, beliefs, or characteristics of a group of people. Surveys can be a useful part of a Web site assessment project. This chapter provides a basic overview of surveys, covering:

- reasons for doing surveys
- advantages and disadvantages of surveys; their relationship to other usability techniques
- how to carry out a survey
- resources for further reading

Reasons for Doing Surveys

Surveys are usually carried out to gather information needed to support decision making. A library might conduct a survey to:

- determine the demand for a planned product or service
- improve an existing service
- find how users rate the library's current products or services
- identify unmet user needs
- discover problems with existing products or services
- use library resources more effectively
- gather input for strategic planning

When done as part of a usability study of a library Web site, the survey should be done at the beginning to help set the parameters and direction of any redesign. A redesign should not be based solely on the results of a survey. Formal usability testing and, if possible, other usability techniques should be used as well.

Surveys can be combined effectively with focus group interviews; problems identified in a survey can be probed in-depth in focus group interviews.

Alternatively, surveys can be used to determine how widespread concerns raised in focus group interviews are among the entire user population.

Advantages and Disadvantages of Surveys

Surveys offer significant advantages. They can be used to gather information from large numbers of people in a relatively short period of time. They can tell you about characteristics of your users: Demographics, how often they use library services, and their attitudes towards library services. When done properly, the results of a survey of a small sample of the user population can accurately represent the results that would have been obtained by surveying all of them.

Surveys also have inherent disadvantages. They are less useful at answering qualitative, or "why," questions; for example, why your users like or dislike a particular library service. Focus group interviews are better at gathering qualitative information, as they allow followup questions and probing of responses. Also, it can be a challenge to select survey samples that are representative of the entire group of interest and therefore avoid bias. Furthermore, designing questions that are clear and gather the desired information may take time. Finally, thorough analysis of survey results may require advanced statistical techniques; for most surveys, basic analytic tools will be adequate.

Steps in Survey Design

Effective survey design involves the following steps:

1. Articulate survey goals.
2. Decide who to survey.
3. Decide how to administer the survey.
4. Develop the survey questions.
5. Pretest the survey.
6. Conduct the survey.
7. Analyze the results and document the findings.

Articulate Survey Goals

Drafting and writing down a concise statement of the survey goals is an invaluable first step. Some questions to consider:

- Why are you thinking of doing a survey?
- What do you hope to learn from the survey?
- Is a survey the best tool for gathering the needed information?
- What additional steps will be required to accomplish the goal?

The statement of the survey goals will be helpful when drafting the survey questions, selecting those to be surveyed, and in determining how the survey will be conducted and the results analyzed.

20

Decide Who to Survey

The group of people from whom information is sought is known as the population of interest, or target population. In a library, the target population might be everyone the library is meant to serve, or alternatively, those actually using the library. If the target population is small enough and the identity of its members known, every member of the target population can be surveyed. This is known as a census survey. When the identity of all the members is unknown, or where the target population is too large for a census survey to be practical, a portion—or sample—of the population is surveyed. If the sample is properly selected, survey results represent with a high degree of accuracy the responses that would have been obtained from surveying the entire target population.

There are two key issues to address when selecting a survey sample: The method to use to select the sample, and how many to sample.

Sample Selection

There are several ways to select a survey sample.

1. *Random sample:* A random sample is one in which the probability of a given member of the target population being surveyed is equal to that of every other member, ensuring that those surveyed are representative of the target population. According to one author, "Freedom from bias is the most important characteristic of a good sample" (Pyrczak, 2006). If those selected to be in the sample are not representative of the population as a whole, bias can occur and the results may be inaccurate. A well-known example of survey bias is that of the *Literary Digest*. Prior to the 1936 U.S. presidential election, it mailed out millions of postcards asking people's preference. It sent the postcards to persons listed in the telephone directories and vehicle registration lists. These people were more affluent and tended to vote Republican—a built-in bias. Based on over 2 million responses, it predicted Alf Landon would win. George Gallup conducted a much smaller survey with a scientifically selected representative sample and correctly predicted Roosevelt's landslide victory.

A random sample requires a list of all the members of the target population from which the people to be surveyed can be selected at random. Random samples can be obtained by drawing names blindfolded out of a hat or by using a random-number table (Pyrczak, 2006).

2. *Systematic sample:* A systematic sample selects every nth person from a list of the members of the target population. The number of persons on the list is divided by the desired sample size to obtain n. Then choose a starting point on the list at random and select every nth name. This technique will normally approach random results.

3. *Stratified sample:* A stratified sample is used when the target population is composed of several subgroups with differing characteristics, such as

21

faculty and students, to ensure an adequate number of responses from each group. Stratified sampling randomly selects from each of the subgroups a number of individuals to be surveyed in proportion to their numbers in the target population.

4. *Convenience sample:* A convenience sample is one that surveys whoever is easily available, for example, by putting a link to the survey on the library Web site, or handing out surveys to persons present in the library. This type of survey can provide useful information, but the results should not be viewed as being representative or statistically valid, as there is no way of knowing how closely those who took the survey resemble the target population.

Sample Size

Alreck and Settle (1985) recommend surveying a minimum of 30 participants and a maximum of 10 percent of the target population, or 1,000—whichever is less. A larger sample is desirable when the decision that needs to be made is important and costly or the target population is diverse. Conversely, if the decision is less important, the population is relatively homogeneous, or only rough estimates are needed, a smaller sample size is usually adequate.

While it is true that the greater the number of responses, the more useful information one is likely to get (particularly if the survey has a section for comments), increasing the sample size runs into the law of diminishing returns. For example, quadrupling the number of responses from 264 to 1,067 only doubles the validity of the results (Suskie, 1996). For national opinion surveys, a sample size of 1,500 is considered adequate (Pyrczak, 2006).

Methods for Administering Surveys
There are several ways surveys can be conducted.

One on One
An interviewer conducts the survey, either in person or on the phone. Advantages of this method are that one is more likely to get an answer to every question as respondents are less likely to skip questions, and the interviewer can explain questions that are not clear to the person being surveyed. Disadvantages are that people may not answer sensitive questions truthfully or may give answers they think will please the interviewer or that are socially acceptable. Also, one-on-one surveys take the most time, which adds significantly to costs.

By Mail or E-mail
Advantages of mail and e-mail surveys are that people are more likely to answer sensitive questions truthfully (as long as they are convinced their responses will be kept confidential), and that they can be conducted more quickly than

one-on-one surveys. Disadvantages include the inability to clarify questions, and, typically, low response rates.

Internet

Internet surveys have a number of advantages: They are fast and easy to conduct, respondents are more likely to answer sensitive questions truthfully, and people tend to provide lengthier comments in Internet surveys than in mail surveys. If needed, Internet surveys allow linking to a page or service respondents are being asked about. Survey tools such as Zoomerang and Survey-Monkey are available online by subscription at relatively low cost, make creating Internet surveys easy, and compile the results automatically. A potential disadvantage is that Internet surveys introduce some bias, because respondents are necessarily computer users and thus may not be representative of the target population.

Developing Survey Questions

Getting the information needed to accomplish the survey's goals requires that the right questions be asked. Good survey questions possess three qualities: Focus, brevity, and clarity. Every question should focus on a single issue or topic and be designed to gather a single piece of information. Questions should be brief; long questions are harder for respondents to process and more likely to be misunderstood. Questions should be designed to be clear to the least fluent members of the sample, such as those who are not native speakers of English. To ensure maximum brevity and clarity, questions should be reviewed by persons other than those who drafted them.

23

General Guidelines

- Keep the survey as brief as possible—aim for a survey that takes no more than 10–15 minutes to complete. Long surveys can be daunting to respondents, who may start skipping questions or answer them without giving them much thought.
- Avoid jargon—for example, words such as ILS, database, and serial—because there is little opportunity to clarify such terminology. A survey respondent who answers without understanding the question won't provide usable information.
- Begin with an introduction stating the purpose of the survey, ask those being surveyed for their help, and thank them.
- Questions should move from general to specific and from easy to hard. Taking a survey is typically an intrusion, and many people have reservations about giving information to strangers. By making the survey easy at the beginning, respondents are likely to get into a rhythm and answer more

difficult questions later in the survey. Group questions in sections, with transitions.

• Provide contact information at the end. This allows survey respondents to clarify questions they might have, or report problems with the survey.

• Ask for demographic information at the end, unless needed to qualify respondents. For example, if you are only interested in surveying current users of a service, you would need to ask "Have you ever used the x service?" as your first question and excuse nonusers from taking the survey.

Types of Questions

There are two basic types of survey questions: Structured and unstructured. Structured, or closed-ended, questions set the format of the response, such as yes or no, multiple choice, or asking for a number ("How many years have you worked in the library?").

In unstructured, or open-ended, questions, respondents are asked to supply free-form answers to questions, for instance, "If you could change one thing about the library, what would it be?" or "Is there anything else you'd like to tell us?"

Most of the survey should consist of structured questions because the information they gather can be more easily analyzed, as responses are comparable, and because they are easier to answer, as they show the type of response being sought. There are several categories of structured questions.

List of categories:

This type of question, also called multiple choice, provides options to choose from. It is important that all possible options should be included.

Examples:

"What is your status?

[   ] Student; [   ] Faculty; [   ] Staff; [   ] Other (please specify _____)"

"Do you have Internet access to the library at home?   [   ] Yes; [   ] No"

Rating:

Rating questions allow respondents to express their opinion on a scale.

Examples:

"How useful is the library's 'Ask a Librarian' service to you?

[   ] Not useful at all; [   ] Minimally useful;

[   ] Moderately useful; [   ] Very useful"

"On a scale of 1 to 5, with 1 being "Don't use" and 5 being "Use regularly," rate how often you use the following library services:

____ ILL

____ Ask-a-Librarian

____ WorldCat

____ The library catalog

Agreement:

Agreement questions ask respondents to express how strongly they agree or disagree with a statement.

Example:

	Strongly disagree	Disagree	No opinion	Agree	Strongly agree
Library collections in my area of study are adequate	☐	☐	☐	☐	☐
I prefer to access library materials online rather than in print	☐	☐	☐	☐	☐
The number of hours the library is open meets my needs	☐	☐	☐	☐	☐

This matrix presents information compactly, which can be helpful when used sparingly but can be difficult for survey respondents in large doses.

Issues Related to Survey Questions

- Responses provided to questions should be mutually exclusive. The response choices '1–10,' '10–20,' and '20 or more' present problems for those whose response is 10 or 20. '1–10,' '11–20,' and '21 or more' is preferable.
- Responses provided should cover all possible cases. Questions that do not allow respondents to give exact responses will be frustrating. One way to cover all possible cases is to provide "Don't know" or "Other" options.
- Demographic questions should be put at the end, unless you are only looking for a particular type of respondent. They are more likely to be answered at the end, especially if the questions are perceived as intrusive (e.g., relating to age or income level); by the end, respondents will be in a pattern of answering.
- In an Internet survey, allow adequate space for comments. A Web survey form with inadequate space for comments will frustrate respondents whose comments are cut short and prevent you from getting useful information. Comments on surveys can provide unexpected insights.
- One source of survey error is habituation. If the survey has a series of questions whose answers are structured identically, users may select the same option for multiple questions. One way to address this is to change the answer format or direction of the scale (1 is best vs. 1 is worst). This will make it more likely respondents will address the questions independently.
- A related issue, when using a Likert scale (where respondents record their degree of agreement or disagreement with a statement, ranging from "Strongly disagree" to "Strongly agree"), is whether to include a neutral option, "Neither agree nor disagree." Some prefer to eliminate the neutral option and force respondents to state an opinion. Others believe the neutral option may reflect

25

the respondent's view, and that forcing the respondent to choose may not yield an accurate representation of the respondent's opinion.

Pretesting the Survey

Pretest the survey with two or three members of the survey's target population. Pretesting will reveal potential problems that could keep it from yielding useful information, such as questions or instructions that are unclear. If doing a Web survey, test it on a variety of browsers to make sure there are no unexpected display problems that would impact potential respondents.

Conducting the Survey

If you are surveying a predetermined sample via mail, e-mail, or Internet, you will want to send out prenotification letters or e-mail messages to let people know the survey is coming. The message should ask the individual to help by taking the survey, explain the reason for the survey, when it is being done, who is sponsoring the survey, what the benefit will be, and the confidentiality policy (if applicable). Some research shows that letters coming from the head of the organization, e.g., library director, result in higher participation rates (Walonick, 2004). If an incentive for answering the survey, such as a prize, is being offered, describe it in the message, along with any impact this will have on confidentiality.

Several days after the survey has been delivered, a message thanking the survey participants and reminding them to complete and return the survey should be sent out.

Analyzing Survey Results

Typically, survey results are entered into a spreadsheet. Tools like Zoomerang and SurveyMonkey automate this process and provide different views of your data; if preferred, results can be downloaded for further analysis. For close-ended questions, assign a code (student=1; faculty=2), with a key explaining the coding used for each question. For open-ended survey responses, identify common themes and exceptions.

Tables

The most commonly used tools for analyzing survey results are frequency tables and cross-tabulation tables. Figure 3.1 is an example of a frequency table showing the numbers and percentages of respondents by academic status.

Cross-tabulation tables, another commonly used technique, show the relationship of two categories. Figure 3.2 is an example of a cross-tabulation table showing perceived usefulness of a library service by academic status.

Figure 3.1: Frequency Table

Category	Frequency	Percent
Undergraduate student	87	77.0%
Graduate student	13	11.5%
Faculty	9	8.0%
Other	4	3.5%
Total	113	100.0%

Figure 3.2: Cross-Tabulation Table

	Not useful at all	Limited usefulness	No opinion	Moderately useful	Very useful
Undergrads	1 (0%)	49 (16%)	10 (3%)	158 (52%)	88 (29%)
Grads	1 (2%)	6 (13%)	1 (2%)	19 (42%)	18 (40%)
Faculty	0 (0%)	1 (9%)	0 (0%)	3 (27%)	7 (64%)

27

Conclusion

Surveys are a technique for gathering information about characteristics, opinions, habits, and behaviors of a group by asking questions of some or all of the members. Surveys can provide quick, statistically reliable information if done properly, but can take time to design, as well as care to ensure that reliable results are obtained. When done to improve the usability of a Web site, they should be done early in the usability assessment process, in conjunction with formal usability testing and other usability techniques.

References

Alreck, Pamela, and Robert Settle. 1985. *The Survey Research Handbook*. Homewood, IL: R. D. Irwin.

Pyrczak, Fred. 2006. *Making Sense of Statistics*. 4th ed. Glendale, CA: Pyrczak.

Rea, Louis M., and Richard A. Parker. 2005. *Designing and Conducting Survey Research: A Comprehensive Guide*. 3rd ed. San Francisco, CA: Jossey-Bass.

Suskie, Linda A. 1996. *Questionnaire Survey Research: What Works*. 2nd ed. Tallahassee, FL: Association for Institutional Research.

Walonick, David S. 2004. *Survival Statistics: Designing and Using Surveys.* Bloomington, MN: StatPac, Inc. Available: www.statpac.com/surveys/surveys.doc (accessed October 19, 2007).

Chapter 4

Focus Group Interviews

Megan Johnson

Introduction

Focus groups are in-depth interviews with a small number of carefully selected people designed to help develop an idea or specific service. They are directed discussions lasting one to two hours and are usually comprised of 6–12 people with a moderator who leads the discussion by asking open-ended questions. In library settings, focus groups are often used to explore perceptions of, and gather opinions on, Web interfaces and patron needs.

Focus groups can be used to discover users' attitudes towards existing or planned interfaces or services. They can gather a wide range of information in a relatively short time and are a good way to find out what users would like. For example, a focus group consisting of current students may reveal that students find it difficult to navigate the interlibrary loan Web pages. This insight suggests that the students need a better designed interlibrary loan interface and provides support for spending the time to improve that process.

It is important to understand focus group interviews in order to use them effectively. Focus groups provide qualitative rather than quantitative data. The results of focus group discussions cannot be generalized or treated statistically, as the number of participants is usually statistically too small to represent a valid sample of the user population.

Some believe that focus groups are not a good way to gather information. Malcolm Gladwell, the author of *Blink*, is quoted in *Advertising Age*: "There is very little psychological justification for the notion that you can find out what people think about an idea—particularly a revolutionary new idea—by asking them" (Thompson and Halliday, 2005: 4). In the same article, Ed Razek, chief creative officer at Limited Brands' Victoria's Secret, says, "Customers can't tell you what they want because they haven't seen it" (Thompson and Halliday, 2005: 4). Although this may be true for innovative products, many library users are familiar with online interfaces or services and can offer valuable, in-depth insights.

Focus groups are a good way to identify problems with a Web site, but they are not always a good way to find solutions to Web site design problems. Focus group participants will not necessarily have the expertise needed to offer the best solution. For example, they may not know what a content management system is or how such a system would improve the library's Web site.

Unlike surveys or posting a question to an electronic discussion forum, focus groups have the added strength of allowing interaction between participants. A skilled moderator will follow up participants' comments with questions geared to find out why users like or dislike something, and also allow new views to surface. Since there is no pressure to reach a consensus, all opinions can be encouraged and aired. In a survey, users may give off-the-cuff answers, but in a focus group setting participants can think in-depth about a topic. Both the interaction between the participants and the sequencing of the questions (from general to specific) can promote this. Focus groups also are helpful when used in conjunction with surveys. If your library has identified concerns through the use of a patron survey, a moderator can follow up with a focus group to clarify issues and test ideas for solutions.

What about alternatives, such as using an electronic discussion forum or group chat for a version of a focus group? Collecting a group of potential users, testing a service like IM reference, then following up with a discussion in group chat is an appropriate way to gather user feedback, but it is not the same thing as a focus group. Electronic discussion forums provide valuable feedback about new ideas or services, but the members of these lists have self-selected to participate because of their interest in a particular topic, and are not your library's "typical" user. However, Nielsen (1997: n.p.) points out, "Although online forum discussions are unlikely to reflect the average user's concerns, they can be a good way of getting in touch with 'power users.'" These users have needs that will sometimes surface later for the average user. When planning for a focus group, an electronic discussion forum may be a good way to solicit ideas or get the group's feedback on ideas.

How to Conduct a Focus Group

The steps in conducting a focus group include:

a) determining your purpose and budget
b) choosing participants
c) developing relevant questions
d) scheduling and facilitating the meeting
e) analyzing the results

30

Determining Your Purpose and Budget

Start the planning process for a focus group by writing a purpose statement, such as "We are conducting a focus group to gather opinions about 'X' and the results will be used to . . ." Consider whether a focus group is the right tool, and whether other or additional tools, such as surveys and observational user testing, should also be employed.

It is important to have a clear idea of your budget. Focus groups are labor-intensive projects; time may be the most expensive item. It takes considerable time to plan the sessions, recruit volunteers, develop your questions, and assess the results. If you hire a professional moderator, there could be a considerable monetary expense. Other items, including honorariums for participants, refreshments, and videotaping, can also add to the cost.

While it adds to the expense, offering an honorarium provides an incentive for potential participants and can make it easier to recruit group members. Honorariums help compensate participants for their time and convey the message that you take their input seriously. They need not be expensive to be effective. Consider giving participants gift certificates to the university bookstore, $10 to $20 an hour, or holding the session over lunch and providing a meal.

When writing about focus groups, a number of authors, including the American Statistical Association, recommend using a trained moderator to lead the discussion. Unless you hire an independent consultant to do this, you need to build the skills to moderate a focus group, or recruit an experienced neutral colleague. It is essential that the moderator clearly understands the topic at hand and the purpose of the focus group. To help maintain objectivity, the moderator should not be too closely involved with the topic under discussion. If conducting a general library focus group, try to avoid selecting a moderator who works at the library. Participants may not provide a frank response if they are concerned about offending the library employee.

31

Selecting Participants

Whom do you invite to participate? This depends on what you are trying to learn. Whether you are thinking about offering a new service or constructing a new building, carefully choose your membership and perhaps plan several groups. If gathering data on the library Web site, which is used differently by different groups, several focus groups may be the most effective option: One for staff, another for freshmen, one for graduate students, and one for teaching faculty.

A benefit of having homogeneous groups is that it facilitates the discussion. If you mix people with different jobs or status, such as administrators and staff or faculty and undergrads, there is the potential for one group to be intimidated and not participate fully. Also, since focus groups are small, having members from a homogeneous group simplifies the analysis of the data collected. If you interview only freshmen in one group and only faculty in a second focus group, you can contrast more easily the responses from these different patron types.

After you identify your target audiences, solicit volunteers in any way that works locally, whether by mailing, posters, or phone calls. Explain the purpose of the focus group interview, when it is being held, the time commitment, and if there is any remuneration. Recruiting participants can be a challenge. After a participant has agreed to come, follow up with a reminder by e-mail or phone in the days before the session. Remember that the target size of a focus group is 6–12 participants. If there are too few participants, ideas and interaction may be limited, and if there are too many, it may be hard for everyone to participate fully. Finally, many universities have an approval process for testing with humans subjects; if so, complete the paperwork for appropriate approval or exemption.

Developing Relevant Questions

The questions a moderator asks will depend on the purpose of the focus group. For example, if the purpose is to determine how best to structure a new service, like a one-on-one research program for students writing a thesis, you may recruit a group of rising seniors, describe the goal, and then ask the students how they would structure the program. Or the moderator can provide the group with a description of the service and then ask specific questions like, "Should students be automatically assigned a research advisor, or should they have to sign up for one? Should we request students do some initial research before they come in for the one-on-one instruction? How should we express that on the request form?" The moderator can supply several wording options as a starting place for that part of the discussion.

To help develop the questions, refer back to the purpose statement to develop six to eight targeted questions that will help discover what you are trying to learn. The moderator should plan the sequence of questions to get everyone involved, first asking factual questions before asking for opinions. The moderator should move from general questions to more specific ones. Make questions as neutral as possible, avoiding the use of disparaging language or enthusiastic descriptions when introducing a topic. For example, if discussing a delivery service, name the service and describe it, if needed, without using adjectives like "popular" or "costly." Make the questions open-ended: If the question can be answered with a yes or no, do not use it.

Be careful in asking "why" questions in following up with a participant in case the respondent feels challenged or defensive. If an answer surprises the moderator, instead of asking, "Why do you think . . ." try using a phrase like, "Can you tell me more about that?" which may elicit a more nuanced response. For the final question, ask respondents if they have any other comments (try a round robin for this). If possible, plan a practice focus group session with librarians or student workers to help the moderator refine the questions. Practice sessions also will help develop or hone the skills of a novice moderator.

Scheduling and Facilitating the Meeting

Schedule a focus group for the beginning stages of a project so you can use the results in the planning process. Hold sessions in a pleasant room free of distractions in a location that is neutral and comfortable for the participants, such as in the student union. Schedule the meetings at a convenient time, perhaps over the lunch hour or early in the evening. Configure chairs in a circle or around a table so that all members can see each other.

Provide name tags and refreshments. The session should begin with introductions from the moderator and recorder (if used). The moderator will welcome the participants and review the purpose of the meeting, explaining to the group what the library wants to learn. If your organization requires consent forms for human testing, have participants sign the necessary forms.

Tell the group how long the meeting will last. Most focus groups run one to two hours. Go over ground rules, such as one person speaks at a time, everyone participates, no side conversations, and respect the opinions of others. If participants are to receive remuneration, explain how that process will work. Review how the session will be recorded if by audio, video, or note taking. If there is a one-way mirror, clarify who is observing. The moderator should address the terms of confidentiality, spelling out who will have access to answers, videotapes, and recordings and also making clear how the results will be used. The moderator should mention that quotes may be used in the report as in "subject A said," but specific names will not be given. Before the moderator begins the discussion, ask participants if they have any questions. Do not run over the time limit unless the whole group still wants to talk.

It is important to record the discussion to facilitate subsequent analysis and sharing of the findings. Options include flip charting, audio and video recordings, and/or a non-participating observer taking notes. Flip charting is a particularly useful tool, as the recorder can ask the speaker if ideas have been captured correctly, one can tally how many participants agree with a statement or use a service, and the notes can be used after the session to group or categorize responses.

Should you tape the meeting? It adds cost and complexity to use a video camera, but it allows others a chance to view the results later. It also can help

33

the moderators build their skills (for example, did they raise their eyebrows or frown at a comment?). The downside of a video recorder is that it may make participants self-conscious. Sound recording is easier, cheaper, and less obtrusive, with many of the same benefits of video recording (with the exception that sound recordings do not capture body language). If you do not record the event, it is advisable to have a non-participating observer in the room or behind a mirror taking notes.

What skills does a moderator need? Effective moderators keep the discussion focused and address all the necessary material in the time allotted. They encourage discussion without influencing the answers. A good moderator ensures that each person in the group participates and interacts with the others, and that the discussion is not dominated by one or two individuals. The moderator will not allow one participant to interrupt or finish another's answer.

The moderator keeps control of the interview and maintains momentum. If the conversation gets off topic, he or she can use phrases like, "that is an interesting point, but let's stay focused on . . ." If someone is not participating, the moderator should directly ask their opinion. Before moving off a topic, they should make sure all opinions have been heard and explored.

The moderator remains neutral and encourages responses with occasional nods of the head, and phrases like "uh huh." He or she steers the discussion using phrases like, "we've been talking about desktop delivery, and now I'd like to move on to the format of the documents." The moderator should not correct misstatements or use the meeting to instruct or educate the participants. Many librarians find it difficult to develop this last skill.

At the end of the session, the moderator will thank the members, remind them that their input was informative and helpful, and restate how the day's results will be used. The moderator should tell participants how to get in touch later if they have further thoughts.

Analyzing the Results

Immediately after the session, while memories are clear, write up a short summary of the session. If using a recorder or observer, debrief and discuss collaboratively. In this initial session, include anything that was not expected with relevant quotes. Consider the scenario of planning for a new online tutorial. You may expect participants will prefer a flash video version with audio. Instead, half the participants agree that an HTML text-based tutorial works best. Record this surprising result with a supporting quote from a subject like, "The speaker in the video spoke too slowly. I read faster than she read, so I was bored."

In the days following the session, continue to analyze and document the results. Even if you are not producing a formal report, some sort of record will be helpful in tracking results. Consider organizing results in a chart, with the questions asked and the number of positive/negative responses, supplemented with quotes demonstrating the opinion. Alternately, organize your results by theme, either with bullet points or in a narrative style. For instance, if you are analyzing a session regarding two different versions of a new Web site, categorize by themes like "link terminology," "placement of search boxes," and "navigation structure." Organize the expressed opinions with quotations under each theme.

In a final report, state conclusions and compare and contrast results from different groups. For example, in a new OPAC design, note that librarians wanted the opening page to be the advanced search page, whereas undergraduates preferred the basic search with a single search box. Include supporting comments and quotations to illustrate each perspective.

Conclusion

Focus group interviews are directed discussions with small groups, preferably 6–12 individuals. Focus group interviews are useful for gathering opinions and perceptions of existing or planned products or services. Planning is a critical success factor, and the moderator plays an important role in the effectiveness of the session. Results of focus group interviews are qualitative rather than quantitative, and should be supplemented with other techniques such as surveys or observational usability testing.

35

References

Nielsen, Jakob. 1997. "The Use and Misuse of Focus Groups." Available: www.useit.com/papers/focusgroups.html

Thompson, Stephanie, and Jean Halliday. 2005. "'Tipping Point' Guru Takes on Focus Groups: Ad Creatives Big Fans of Gladwell's Call to Rely on Gut Instincts." *Advertising Age* 76, no. 4: 4–5.

Helpful Web Sites

American Statistical Association. "What Are Focus Groups?" Pamphlet. Available: www.amstat.org/sections/srms/brochures/focusgroups.pdf

Greenbaum, Tom. Various dates. Focus group articles. Available: www.groupsplus.com/pages/articles.htm (revised December 10, 2003).

McNamara, Carter. 2006. "Basics of Conducting Focus Groups." Available: www.mapnp.org/library/evaluatn/focusgrp.htm

Six Sigma. Various dates. "Focus Groups." Available: www.isixsigma.com/vc/focus_groups/

University of Surrey. 1997. "Focus Groups." *Social Research Update* 19 (Winter). Available: http://sru.soc.surrey.ac.uk/SRU19.htm

Chapter 5

Card Sorting

Terry Nikkel
and Shelley McKibbon

Introduction

One of the most important elements of the library Web site design process is determining how information and resources will be organized on the site. It is crucial to get user feedback as early as possible to ensure that the final navigation scheme, which exposes the relationships between site resources and features, is practical and usable. Card sorting is a procedure used early in the design process to develop an understanding of how users themselves perceive and categorize library collections and services. It can dramatically improve Web site taxonomies and ultimately the usability of the entire Web site.

Library Web designers tend to categorize their sites using labels that are meaningful to them, but which frequently baffle typical users. Furthermore, many library Web sites are organized around administrative functions, for example, "circulation"—a meaningless category to users who may not know that the term refers to the processes and policies surrounding the borrowing of materials from the library. Many users approach library Web sites with a specific task in mind; for instance, finding information on a research topic, determining library hours and locations, or perhaps seeing what library employment opportunities are available. Web site designers need to be mindful that most users are not familiar with the inner workings of the library, and thus library Web site navigation and terminology need to be carefully thought out to avoid misunderstanding and user frustration. Card sorting is an efficient, economical, and quick way to reveal problems and in turn discover solutions.

Process

Card sorting studies range from informal exercises to highly structured and rigorously controlled research, but the basic design for all is quite similar. Subjects, who represent user groups like undergraduate students, young adults, researchers, and so on, are recruited and asked to sort cards bearing labels and

37

titles corresponding to library services, collections, and titles into groupings that seem logical and appropriate to them. Participants are then asked to create their own labels for these groups. Analysis of these groupings and labels is often highly informative and results in relevant and useful suggestions for improved Web site organization and navigation.

A card sorting study begins with the creation of a set of cards that represents the information contained on or proposed for a Web page or site. Three-by-five index cards are fine, but slips of paper cut to size serve equally well. Names of services and resources are printed on individual cards and include things like reference assistance, document delivery, library hours and contact information, along with important collections (catalog, theses, electronic resources, etc.), plus a sampling of titles of major reference works, journals, and databases in broad areas or specific disciplines. Large Web sites may require as many as 150–200 cards, which will take a typical user about an hour to sort and label.

Digital simulations of card sorting exercises do exist, and are useful in large studies, but manual sorting of real cards is preferred in small-scale studies because of the ease of setup and administration. In any size of study, analysis can be greatly aided by tools such as Microsoft Excel, which allows individual responses to be grouped with others easily and quickly to reveal patterns that can ultimately lead to improvements in Web site design.

Methodology

Like many studies, card sorting is as much a logistical as an analytical challenge, but one of the many appealing features of this approach to understanding user needs is that just about any size of the study will yield good results. The first tasks are selecting the labels for the cards and recruiting participants. Assuming a team is involved in conducting the study (though a team is not absolutely necessary for a small-scale exercise), these tasks can be split up and accomplished quickly. Most cards should reflect current resources and services. If new ones are being considered for inclusion in the new or revised site, add these to test them as well. Participants are recruited in the usual ways; for example, posters, class announcements, advertisements, and so on (see Chapter 9). The offer of an incentive (a small cash payment or perhaps a gift of some kind) is needed sometimes to get users involved. Participants are told that the activity is not a test, and that there are no right or wrong answers.

A card sorting session with a participant may be divided into three steps: Initial sorting, grouping, and labeling. In the first stage, each participant is given a set of labeled cards and three "place mats." The mats (laminated 8.5 × 11 sheets of paper can be used) are labeled "resources used at least once," "resources recognized but not used," and "resources not recognized." The subject is instructed to sort the cards into these categories, with the place mats serving to help them keep the three piles separate. After sorting the cards, the participant is given blank cards and asked to add any resources he or she has used but that were not represented by one of the prelabeled cards.

After finishing the initial sort, the participant is given a pen and asked to label the cards in their "resources used at least once" pile according to frequency of usage. The frequency categories can be something like daily (marked with the label daily [d], weekly [w], and occasionally or at least once [o]). While the participant is doing this, the moderator marks the other two piles of cards as either known but not used [k] or not recognized [?]. Having participants label their cards in this way will allow the team to detect any patterns in the resources that are or are not used. The pile marked with the [?], or not recognized, is set aside.

In the second step, the participant sorts the "resources used at least once" cards into what he or she considers logical groupings. All cards representing resources used by the subject must be included in this sort. Participants can be given the option to sort any or all of the "resources known but not used" cards; they may know, for example, that *The New England Journal of Medicine* is an electronic journal, but have never had the occasion to use it. The moderator must be careful not to comment on any particular selection; card sorting is designed to determine how the user perceives different resources (or at least the labels used to define them).

Finally, the participant is asked to label the groupings of cards they have created. Using fresh cards of a different color (to help keep category labels distinct from resource cards), the participant writes down a word or phrase that best represents the entire group of cards. The groupings themselves are necessarily completely subjective; this is indeed the point of the study and it cannot be stressed too much. Participants should feel completely free to make up whatever labels they think best describe the groups of cards. Again, the moderator should refrain from coaching or questioning, but it may be necessary at this point to seek clarification of individual labels if it is not clear what they mean.

As each session is completed, the team members record results in a Microsoft Excel spreadsheet that has one worksheet for each participant. All of the resources/services used on the cards should be listed in rows, and there should be a column for the user-created category the item was placed in or, if applicable, either ? for an unknown resource or k for a known but never used resource that was not included in the participant sort. There should also be column for recording frequency of use as indicated by d, w, o, or k (if the resource was never used but recognized and included in the sort). After the spreadsheet is filled in for each participant, the team can sort resources into their user-created categories and look for points of comparison. Do certain resources tend to be grouped together? Do different users choose similar labels for groups of similar resources? There will likely be at least some very obvious general trends that can be used in the Web site design.

Excel can be used to cluster user responses to whether resources were known or not known to gain insight into usefulness of current labels. Not surprisingly, commonly used resources like "Library Hours" and "University Home Page" will have broad recognition, while others like "Proquest Databases" or "Nature (Online)" may be recognized by few, if any, participants. Information like this might lead designers to avoid placing specific titles and types of resources at the same hierarchical level in the Web site navigation scheme. Also, clustering can confirm trends revealed in the labels participants attach to different resources. For example, in a card sorting study conducted at a medium-sized university library, over half of the 26 participants grouped various writing-related resources together (e.g., "Footnotes," "How to Write Essays," and "Citing Sources in Your Writing") and gave them the label "Writing." It had not occurred to designers to include such a category on the top-level page before, but the study revealed that it would be useful, and it has since been included as a main page link. The full card sorting study is reported below.

Case Study: Dalhousie University

Dalhousie University in Halifax, Nova Scotia, Canada has four libraries serving 16,000 undergraduate students, 2,000 graduate students, and 1,500 staff and faculty members. A university-mandated Web site redesign project over three years has seen most university Web pages redeployed with a new look and feel and maintained within a new content management system. The libraries, each of which previously designed, edited, and maintained its own site, amalgamated all four into a single Web site to improve services, navigation, and accessibility for all users. At the start of the library project, the team responsible for seeing through the redesign and implementation decided to turn to users to help inform the entire process.

One of the important elements of the redesign activity was determining how the team would organize the information and resources on the site. The team (called WIT—the Web Implementation Team) decided that it was important to get user feedback regarding the organizational schemes *they* found logical. In order to do this as early in the process as possible, WIT decided to use a card sorting activity.

This study was based on one carried out by a team member when she worked at the University of Texas Southwestern Medical Center in Dallas. It was not intended as a rigorous research study, but rather as a way to let the team gather impressions of what users considered logical systems for organizing information.

WIT generated a list of 185 electronic resources available through the library Web site. This list was largely based on usage, although several subject-specific resources were added by hand in the interest of creating a sample that represented smaller user groups. The list was then used to generate sets of cards, which were used by participants in the sorting activity.

Members of the team posted sign-up sheets in the four university libraries. Members of the team were based at each of these locations, so it was convenient to recruit participants in this way. All participants were volunteers and were given an incentive of $10.00 added to their campus convenience cards. Twenty-six people eventually participated. The team made no effort to gather a scientific sample and simply accepted anyone who signed up (in a later usability test of the real test Web site, the team randomly selected participants representing faculties and groups in proportion).

Each participant met one-on-one with a WIT member. They were given the labeled cards and asked to sort them into three piles: "Resources used at least once," "Resources recognized but not used," and "Resources not recognized." The participants were supplied with sheets to sort the cards onto, ensuring that no confusion arose as to which pile was which.

After the cards were sorted, the participants were asked to take the pile of cards representing resources they used and indicate on the card whether they used the resource daily (d), weekly (w), or "at least once" (o). The WIT member moderating the session marked the other cards as "known but not used" (k) or "not recognized" ($?$).

The participants then took all the cards representing resources they used and sorted them into groupings that made sense to them. If they wished, they could include any of the "known but not used" resources they chose. They did not sort the unknown resources. When they were satisfied with the groupings they had created, the participants used colored cards to label their groups with names that made sense to them.

A spreadsheet was created to allow team members to input the results of each session. The spreadsheet consisted of an alphabetical listing of the resources used on the cards. Each entry included a space in which moderators recorded the user-created category in which the item had been placed (either the category name as recorded on the colored card, x if the named resource was recognized but not used or included in the sort, or $?$ if the named resource was not recognized) and a space in which the frequency of use was recorded (d, w, o, or x if the resource was included in the sort). If the resource was not recognized, the space was left blank, since usage frequency and category were the same.

Once the spreadsheet was filled in, WIT was able to sort resources into their user-created groups and compare them to determine whether certain resources were generally put in the same groups, or whether several participants

41

came up with similar group names. This allowed WIT to look for similarities among participant results. It was observed that stronger, more understandable labels were sorted by more participants into fewer categories, suggesting a high level of confidence that the label was widely recognized, while weaker, less understandable labels were sorted by fewer participants and into more categories, indicating more guesses were being made. Figure 5.1 shows part of a worksheet that sums up the number of participants who included the label in their individual sort; for example, 26 out of 26 participants included the card "Library Hours" in their sort. Clearly, the term was broadly meaningful. On the other hand, only four participants included the card labelled "Electronic Reading Room" in their sort, indicating that the term would not likely be useful as a navigation link or topical heading.

Conclusion

Card sorting is an excellent method for testing the usefulness of links and labels with real users and can help minimize library jargon and other confusing language. Indeed, card sorting can even help keep Web pages current, or at the very least ensure that definitions of resources are clear and unambiguous. In the same study mentioned above, one participant categorized the card labeled "Cell" (a major journal title in health sciences) under "Library Services." When asked to explain, the subject replied that she was able to use her mobile phone anywhere in the library, and thus thought that the library had some kind of enhanced signal, which was a great service!

Figure 5.1: Card Sort Spreadsheet

	Library Hours	Reference Desk Hours	Today's opening times	Library staff phone numbers	Room bookings	Wireless coverage at Dal	Fines	Lending & recall policy	Services for persons w	Campus Map	Document delivery form	Interlibrary loan	Renew a book	Reserves	Remote (Off-Campus)	How do I find other libr	Status of On-Line Res	Borrowing rules for pat	Writing workshop	New acquisitions	Electronic Reading Ro	Change Address For N
Library Hours		26	20	18	18	18	14	12	14	15	12	9	12	10	13	10	12	11	9	9	6	8
Reference Desk Hours	26		20	18	18	18	14	12	14	15	12	9	12	10	13	10	12	11	9	9	6	8
Today's opening times	20	20		16	14	16	13	11	12	13	11	8	10	9	12	9	10	8	8	6	7	
Library staff phone numbers	18	18	16		15	17	14	13	13	13	12	10	10	10	13	11	9	11	10	8	6	8
Room bookings	18	18	14	15		18	13	11	16	12	13	10	14	10	10	8	9	9	10	8	6	7
Wireless coverage at Dal libraries	18	18	16	17	18		14	12	16	15	13	10	11	10	9	10	10	8	6	9	6	8
Fines	14	14	13	14	13	14		16	13	9	14	10	13	12	10	9	10	10	9	9	6	8
Lending & recall policy	12	12	11	13	11	12	16		11	7	13	11	12	10	10	10	9	11	8	7	6	7
Services for persons with disabilities	14	14	12	13	16	16	13	11		10	12	10	13	10	11	8	8	9	11	7	6	8
Campus Map	15	15	13	13	12	15	9	7	10		7	4	7	5	9	6	7	6	7	4	3	5
Document delivery forms	12	12	11	12	13	13	14	13	12	7		13	13	13	9	9	9	8	8	6	6	8
Interlibrary loan	9	9	8	10	10	10	10	11	10	4	13		11	14	8	10	8	8	8	8	7	7
Renew a book	12	12	10	10	14	12	13	12	13	7	13	11		10	10	5	10	8	9	6	6	9
Reserves	10	10	9	10	10	10	12	10	10	5	13	14	10		8	9	8	8	7	10	7	7
Remote (Off-Campus) Access Instructions	13	13	12	13	10	11	10	10	11	9	8	10	8		11	9	9	8	5	5	9	
How do I find other libraries' catalogues?	10	10	9	11	8	10	9	10	8	6	9	10	5	9	11		7	8	8	6	4	5
Status of On-Line Resources	12	12	10	9	9	9	10	9	8	7	9	8	10	8	9	7		6	6	8	5	7

Basic analysis / Final matrix / Reduced matrix / Spectrum \ **Grouped** /

Chapter 6

Paper Prototyping

Nora Dimmock

Introduction

A paper prototype is a representation of a Web page that is printed or drawn on paper. In paper prototype testing, the user interacts with a paper mockup or prototype of the product during usability testing as if it were a functional computer interface. Paper prototyping is an integral part of the iterative design process that allows Web site designers to produce usable designs rapidly and inexpensively. The iterative design process is based on a cycle of designs, where usability informs the improvements to successive versions.

In most situations, a paper prototype is an unsophisticated sketch of the user interface with little or no functionality. The most elaborate paper prototypes are fully designed renderings of a real Web interface including underlying pages in the Web site, allowing the usability tester to show the test participant where they will be taken when they click on a link, button, or navigate in the site. The usability test monitor functions as both the tester and the computer, turning pages when there are multiple prototypes. Where there is just a single interface to be tested, the tester asks participants to elaborate on their choices: "Why did you click on this link? What do you think will happen? Where will this take you?" The information gathered at this stage helps the design team determine if they have a match between the system and the user's expectations or mental models.

While a quick prototype may look unsophisticated in comparison to full-color mockups, it can be a very effective tool in usability testing. In Jared Spool's article, "Looking Back on 16 Years of Paper Prototyping," he writes, "One lesson we've learned is that paper prototypes are ideal for testing the navigation elements of a design. Where they fall short is when we're trying to learn something about content-rich designs . . . when we're interested in the content we'll skip over paper mockups and go straight to evaluating the electronic renditions of the design" (2005: 3).

Paper prototypes are great for testing Web site interfaces, but they also can be used to test the usability of forms, computer programs, and even three-dimensional objects. Testing with a paper prototype is an important methodology for making incremental design improvements quickly. It allows Web site designers to see how users will interact with an interface before committing to the expense and time of writing the underlying code. The speed with which paper prototypes can be produced is an important factor in their value to the iterative design process. "The Web development process must be highly accelerated—'Web time' has become synonymous with headlong desperation and virtually impossible deadlines" (Constantine and Lockwood, 2002: 42).

Paper prototypes can be produced by a Web site design team or by a team that includes designers, programmers, and users. The production of prototypes can be a great tool for bringing the whole team together. One study on the use of prototypes in commercial design teams concluded that prototypes or representations can be the focal point of the software development cycle. "Multi-competence teams are necessary to develop software of the complexity and quality now being routinely requested by clients. The coordination that this incurs, together with an ever increasing use of iterative development centered around prototypes, means that representations take on a key role in facilitating communication between project stakeholders" (Bryan-Kinns and Hamilton, 2002: 98).

Although paper prototyping is a fast and easy way to elicit user input, many design teams do not use it. Jakob Nielsen thinks this is because "people don't think they will get enough information from a method that is so simple and so cheap. It feels like you're cheating" (Nielsen, 2003: 1). In his article "Fast, Cheap Requirements: Prototype, or Else!" author Stephen Andriole writes, "The main lesson we've learned is that throwaway prototyping (sometimes called exploratory prototyping) is always cost effective and always improves specifications" (1994: 85). It may be hard to sell test results to stakeholders when using quick and unsophisticated prototypes, but empirical evidence exists that there is little difference in results between high fidelity and low fidelity prototypes (Virzi et al., 1996). Svanaes and Seland used low-fidelity prototyping in the design of mobile computing systems and justified the validity of their test protocol by applying the same standards used by social scientists to evaluate research: "Most authors agree on basic evaluation criteria such as objectivity, reliability, validity, and transferability" (2004: 485). If your test is carefully designed to focus on your users, and the relevant tasks and situations that they will bring to the Web site, then it will meet all of these standards and allow meaningful data to be collected (Svanaes and Seland, 2004).

Paper Prototype Design

Several studies examined the design of prototypes and their impact on the Web site design process and concluded that designing paper prototypes can have the added benefit of bringing the designers and users together before the design reaches the stage where going back to the drawing board would be prohibitive. Usability professional Jared Spool (2005: 2) says, "group prototyping is key... paper prototyping with large teams gets all the issues on the table, allows everybody to see the user's reactions, and produces a cohesion we rarely find from other project activities."

Bryan-Kinns and Hamilton (2002), who studied the use of prototypes in commercial projects, take this one step further by discussing the value of adding user input to the prototype design itself. "Thus while participatory design techniques have been developed primarily to promote and support user involvement, these techniques have knock-on effects for the design process as a whole: The issues expand from just promoting designer-user communication to supporting designer-designer communication, and designer-programmer communication, and so on" (Bryan-Kinns and Hamilton, 2002: 91). Bellotti and Rogers studied the work practices of several multimedia publishing groups and their reliance on hand-printed and sketched documents and found that "it is simple to move between multiple sketches, schematics and proofs on paper, whereas, online, the manipulation of layered windows and switching between different applications is relatively cumbersome" (1997: 283).

The amount of detail, the quality of the graphics, and the presentation of the prototypes can influence the way test subjects interact with them, which can, in turn, influence test results. Bryan-Kinns and Hamilton (2002) found that their users—commercial Web site design customers—were confused by rough interactive prototypes, or wire frames, viewed through a Web browser. "The prototype at this iterative design stage should have been more coherent in its visual language—either more visually appealing in a Web context, or taken out of the Web browser and viewed in a different context" (Bryan-Kinns and Hamilton, 2002: 97). Their study concludes, "users, as an audience, prefer to use systems that are consistent along the fidelity dimension (i.e., consistent interaction, content, and visual design)" (Bryan-Kinns and Hamilton, 2002: 98). Grady (2000: 39), who also studied usability testing using paper prototypes, found they provide "critical feedback from the users, who appear to be more willing to suggest significant flaws when the site design is obviously very rough."

The fidelity or detail of the prototypes has been the focus of recent studies and research, which supports the use of rapid prototyping early in the design phase where the testing can answer navigational or concept questions. Svanaes and Seland (2004: 480) concluded from their study of prototyping techniques

45

for designing mobile computing systems that "the prototyping materials provided have a strong impact both on the resulting form factor and its imagined functionality." Rettig (1994: 22) stresses the importance of keeping the paper prototype as simple as possible to avoid comment on aesthetic features while "the hand-made appearance of a paper or acetate prototype forces the users to think about content rather than appearance."

Liu and Khooshabeh compared the usability results of both paper and interactive prototypes for ubiquitous computing applications and found "paper prototyping is insufficient for supporting unique Ubicomp requirements, such as scalability, but a prototype with higher fidelity and automation levels can enhance the quality of interaction data available for evaluation" (2003: 1030). The authors also found that the paper prototype testing technique, which uses a human to act as the computer, can give misleading usability results. "Participants saw that the 'computer' only updated a small section of the screen for the overhead view. They would wait until the 'computer' updated the screen to quickly figure out where to go. Participants using the interactive prototype had to pay attention to the whole screen, since they did not have any visual cues to the relevant information on screen" (Liu and Khooshabeh, 2003: 1031). Spool (2000) also cautions about preparing prototypes carefully, as a handwritten element on a printed screenshot could draw attention to that detail.

Usability Testing with Paper Prototypes

Paper prototype tests use the same methodology as other types of usability tests. The steps involved are the same: Identify the user groups, define key tasks, create designs, test the test, and test with users. The most important step in testing with paper prototypes is testing the test, which is essentially the final step in prototype design. Testing the test with members of the design team can reveal flaws in the test methodology, such as poorly worded tasks, unclear language, or missing paper prototypes of important screens or navigational elements, and allow you to fix them before testing with users. This step is particularly important if there is a limited pool of test subjects available, as it allows the tester to practice the physical manipulation of the prototype and testing materials prior to the actual testing. Testing the test does not need to be formal—a quick consultation or practice run with the Web site design team to make sure that the test monitor can recreate the user experience during testing is appropriate.

Identifying user groups will help define key tasks for the Web site or page. For example, when testing a series of search interfaces for finding scholarly articles, there may be more than one intended user group involved. A basic search page may be intended for novice searchers, such as undergraduates, while an advanced search page may be intended for advanced searchers, such as graduate students, faculty, and librarians. The key tasks should reflect the level of sophistication of these users and the tasks they will be performing. A basic search interface task may be to find an article on nuclear war using a basic search interface, while an advanced task may be to find a specific article using an advanced interface that includes field searching. A small task set created by prioritizing user actions will allow you to test the basic functionality of the site without testing features (Ferre et al., 2001).

After determining the user tasks, the next step is to develop the paper prototype. A prototype can be a simple drawing of the interface sketched out in black marker or pen. A variety of stroke widths can be used to emphasize elements of the design, or the entire prototype can be sketched out with the same pen. Links can be underlined if that is a feature of the site, or users can be asked to make assumptions by telling the tester it is a link when they select text or a screen element. Mathew Klee (2000: 3) suggests using "the 'incredibly intelligent mouse'—a fancy way to say we let the user decide what's a link simply by following their behavior." Buttons can be represented by sketched rectangles, areas of text that are not essential to the design can be represented by squiggly lines, and form elements such as text boxes and drop-down menus can be sketched in with default values written in. Post-It notes with drop-down menu choices should be prepared ahead of time. When those elements are selected, the tester can "open up" the menu by pasting the Post-It on the page. Fully rendered graphics of the interface can also be used, but these take more time to produce. Try to anticipate any possible interaction a user may have with the prototype to make the test as authentic as possible by showing them the result of their action. It may be necessary to make prototypes of a number of pages in the site to get accurate test results. When you are satisfied with the prototype designs, try them out by testing with members of the design team using your key tasks. This tests the test, which will make testing with users run more smoothly.

A low-fidelity paper prototype of the University of Rochester's River Campus Libraries Web site is shown in Figure 6.1. This prototype allowed to gather feedback on the navigation and site hierarchy. The Quicklinks feature allowed test subjects to write in their own quick links. Figure 6.2 shows a high-fidelity paper prototype of the home page. Testing this prototype elicited many comments about the color scheme and graphics.

Now you're ready to test with users. Paper prototype testing relies on the same technique to elicit user comment as testing a functional Web site—the think-aloud protocol. The think-aloud protocol encourages users to verbalize their thought processes. A good way to get users comfortable with speaking their thoughts out loud is to have them read the tasks out loud before starting. It is also helpful to remind them that it is the interface or design that is being

Figure 6.1: Low-Fidelity Paper Prototype

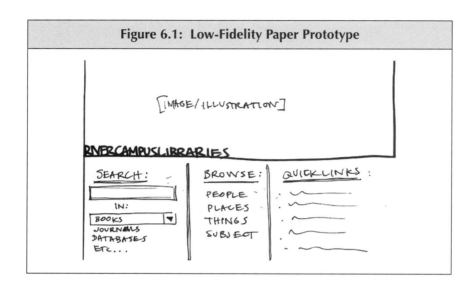

Figure 6.2: High-Fidelity Paper Prototype

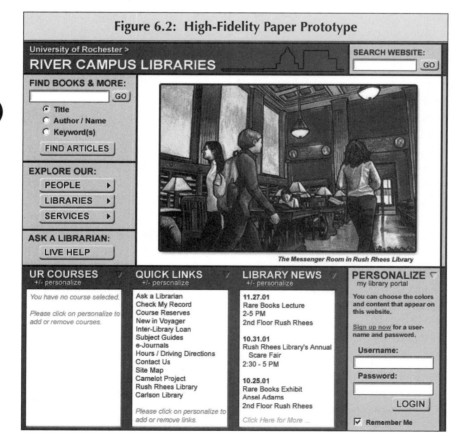

tested, not their skill at Internet searching or computer use. The use of paper prototypes can be an advantage in this respect; users with computer anxiety will be relieved not to have to sit in front of a "live" system, and there is no possibility of system failure.

To get the most from the test, try to approximate the system as much as possible. Use a paper with an hourglass, working symbol, or other text or graphic to represent response time when transitioning between screens if the live system has a long response time between actions. Encourage the user to use their index finger or a pen to represent their mouse clicks and to describe their actions and assumptions as much as possible: "When I click this link I think I'll go to . . ." Try to be as objective as possible. It can be difficult to act as the computer, especially when users ask direct questions. Remind them the tester is the computer and ask them to continue speaking out loud to elicit more information about their problem. For example, in a test where the user asks, "This is searching x database, right?" one could respond "I can't answer that now, remember, I'm the computer, but continue to speak out loud and tell me where you think you are and where you're navigating to so we can design a system that matches your expectations."

If testing forms, have users write their text input directly on the forms; copies of the prototypes will ensure an ample supply of forms for subsequent users. Alternatively, the tester could cover the prototype with transparencies, allowing it to be "refreshed" for the next user. When users select the arrow next to a drop-down box, paste the prepared menu over the text box and have them continue to select menu items. Presenting prototypes of search results pages can be tricky; while the tester cannot predict the search terms entered by users, a prototype of the results page should represent the important elements presented in search results. The average user is usually savvy enough to understand. The Neilsen-Norman Group (2003) has an excellent DVD that demonstrates many of these techniques and shows several live tests.

Presenting Results

Results should be presented in a way that is meaningful to the design team. In the book on paper prototyping, author Carolyn Snyder offers some good advice. "It's important for observers to record data in a form that won't be subject to contentious debate later. It's natural for us to filter information through our own set of ideas and prejudices, but this subjectivity means you're now dealing with opinion rather than data" (2003: 255). Do not report inconclusive results; it will just diminish the effectiveness of clearly discovered flaws in the design. Also, do not infer user actions; ask users for clarification when they pause or hesitate. If the tests have been videotaped or usability software with video/audio presentation software components has been used, presenting clips of the most problematic parts of the user experience can be extremely effective. Since paper prototyping is a rapid iteration technique, brief reports are appropriate.

Conclusion

Paper prototypes can be a valuable addition to your usability program and your Web site design process. They allow you to test incremental improvements to your design quickly and inexpensively. Because testing with a paper prototype allows the design team to cycle through new designs rapidly, major flaws can be caught before they are passed along to the development team, saving both time and money. Mayhew and Bias (2003) compared the cost benefit of paper prototype development to live prototype development and estimated a savings of 80 hours in development, or $14,000.00 at $175.00/hour. Incorporating prototype development into your iterative Web site design process can improve communication among the design team and stakeholders as well. "Developers saw firsthand the difference in people's reactions to successive refinements in their designs. Within days of designing an interface, they saw exactly how their work was perceived by people just like those who will eventually be using their product" (Rettig, 1994: 23).

Paper prototypes can be as simple as a quick sketch of an interface on plain paper with black marker or pen, or as sophisticated as a full graphic rendering of a Web site design. The design of the prototype should take into consideration a number of factors, including the user group, the current stage of development, and the elements of the design you want tested. New prototypes can be designed to address the most important usability issues, and the design can be retested. Beyer and Holtzblatt (1999: 41) sum up the value of paper prototypes succinctly: "Paper prototypes are always popular and always successful. They're quick to build and easy to run. . . . Customers love paper prototypes, because they give customers an opportunity to understand a new design and contribute to it."

References

Andriole, Stephen J. 1994. "Fast, Cheap Requirements: Prototype, or Else!" *IEEE Software* 11, no. 2: 85–87.

Bellotti, Victoria, and Yvonne Rogers. 1997. "From Web Press to Web Pressure: Multimedia Representations and Multimedia Publishing." Paper presented at CHI '97: Proceedings of the SIGCHI Conference on Human Factors in Computing Systems, Atlanta, GA. Available: http://doi.acm.org/10.1145/258549.258755 (accessed May 4, 2007).

Beyer, Hugh, and Karen Holtzblatt. 1999. "Contextual Design." *Interactions* 6, no. 1: 32–42.

Bryan-Kinns, Nick, and Fraser Hamilton. 2002. "One for All and All for One?: Case Studies of Using Prototypes in Commercial Projects." Paper presented at NordiCHI 2002: Proceedings of the Second Nordic Conference on Human-Computer Interaction, Aarhus, Denmark. Available: http://doi.acm.org/10.1145/572020.572032 (accessed May 5, 2007).

Constantine, L. L., and L. A. D. Lockwood. 2002. "Usage-Centered Engineering for Web Applications." *IEEE Software* 19, no. 2: 42–50.

Ferre, X., N. Juristo, H. Windl, and L. Constantine. 2001. "Usability Basics for Software Developers." *IEEE Software* 18, no. 1: 22–29.

Grady, Helen M. 2000. "Web Site Design: A Case Study in Usability Testing Using Paper Prototypes." Paper presented at IPCC/SIGDOC 2000: Proceedings of IEEE Professional Communication Society International Professional Communication Conference and 18th Annual ACM International Conference on Computer Documentation, Cambridge, MA. Available: http://ieeexplore.ieee.org/xpl/freeabs_all.jsp?tp=&arnumber=887259&isnumber=19161 (accessed May 1, 2007).

Klee, Mathew. 2000. "Five Paper Prototyping Tips." *User Interface Engineering* (March 1). Available: www.uie.com/articles/prototyping_tips/ (accessed June 19, 2005).

Liu, Linchuan, and Peter Khooshabeh. 2003. "Paper or Interactive?: A Study of Prototyping Techniques for Ubiquitous Computing Environments." Paper presented at CHI 2003: CHI '03 Extended Abstracts on Human Factors in Computing Systems, Ft. Lauderdale, FL. Available: http://portal.acm.org/citation.cfm?id=766132 (accessed May 3, 2007).

Mayhew, Deborah J., and Ralph G. Bias. 2003. "Cost-Justifying Web Usability." In *Human Factors and Web Development*, ed. Julie Ratner (63–88). Mahwah, NJ: Lawrence Erlbaum Associates.

Moffatt, Karyn, Joanna McGrenere, Barbara Purves, and Maria Klawe. 2004. "The Participatory Design of a Sound and Image Enhanced Daily Planner for People with Aphasia." Paper presented at CHI 2004. Proceedings of the SIGCHI Conference on Human Factors in Computing Systems, Vienna, Austria. Available: http://portal.acm.org/citation.cfm?id=985744 (accessed May 1, 2007).

Nielsen, Jakob. 2003. "Paper Prototyping: Getting User Data Before You Code." Jakob Nielsen's Alertbox (April 14). Available: www.useit.com/alertbox/20030414.html (accessed June 21, 2005).

Nielsen-Norman Group. 2003. *Paper Prototyping: A How-To Video*. Available: www.nngroup.com/reports/prototyping/

Rettig, Marc. 1994. "Prototyping for Tiny Fingers." *Communications of the ACM* 37, no. 4: 21–27.

Snyder, Carolyn. 2003. *Paper Prototyping: The Fast and Easy Way to Design and Refine User Interfaces*. San Francisco, CA: Morgan Kaufmann.

Spool, Jared M. 2005. "Looking Back on 16 years of Paper Prototyping." *User Interface Engineering* (July 27). Available: www.uie.com/articles/looking_back_on_paper_prototyping/ (accessed May 25, 2007).

51

———. 2000. "Five Paper Prototyping Tips." *User Interface Engineering* (March 1). Available: www.uie.com/articles/prototyping_tips/ (accessed May 21, 2007).

Svanaes, Dag, and Gry Seland. 2004. "Putting the Users Center Stage: Role Playing and Low-Fi Prototyping Enable End Users to Design Mobile Systems." Paper presented at CHI 2004, Vienna, Austria. Proceedings of the SIGCHI Conference on Human Factors in Computing Systems. Available: http://delivery.acm. org/10.1145/990000/985753/p479-svanaes.pdf?key1=985753&key2= 3503701811&coll=GUIDE&dl=GUIDE,ACM&CFID=24728192&CFTOKEN= 35962246 (accessed May 1, 2007).

Virzi, R. A., J. L. Sokolov, and D. Karis. 1996. "Usability Problem Identification Using Both Low- and High-Fidelity Prototypes." In *Proceedings of the SIGCHI Conference on Human Factors in Computing Systems: Common Ground* (Vancouver, British Columbia, Canada, April 13–18), ed. M. J. Tauber (236–243). New York: ACM Press.

Usability Testing
Tom Lehman

Introduction

The term "usability testing" can be used to describe a variety of methods used to assess the usability of a Web site. Card sorting exercises, heuristic evaluations, and focus group interviews are all usability methods used to gather information relating to the usability of a Web site. In this chapter, the term usability testing is used to describe what has also been called user testing (Nielsen, 2003), formal usability testing (Battleson, Booth and Weintrop, 2001), basic usability testing (University of Washington Libraries, 2005), user protocols (Covey, 2002), or task-based testing (Kirkwood, 2007)—the process of observing test participants carry out specified tasks as a means of testing the usability of the Web site.

Usability testing differs from other usability techniques in that it lets the test administrator see what users actually do, not what they say they do; usability tests provide real data as opposed to opinion or conjecture. Each usability technique has its strengths and weaknesses; a comprehensive assessment program will incorporate several techniques. According to Nielsen (2003), usability testing is the most basic and useful technique for studying usability; Battleson et al. (2001: 189) state that "[t]he most effective means of assessing a site's usability is with usability testing." If limitations on time or resources permit just one usability method to be used, it should be usability testing.

There are three phases to usability tests: (1) preparing for the usability test; (2) conducting the usability test; and (3) analyzing the results of the usability test and preparing a report and recommendations. These phases are discussed in detail below.

Preparing for the Usability Test

Develop a Usability Test Plan

The first step in preparing for a usability test is developing a usability test plan. Having a usability test plan guides the design of the test and increases the likelihood that the test results will provide the desired information. Usability test plans can range from simple to elaborate. The key elements are:

1. The reason the test is being done, which determines the information that will be needed and governs the design of the test.
2. The user population that will be tested.
3. The tasks that will be performed.
4. Test design: How it will be conducted and how the results will be recorded.

Web site usability tests are conducted for a variety of reasons:

1. To determine problems with the Web site. This type of usability test, known as an *assessment* test, is most appropriate at the beginning of a design or assessment phase. It is the most common type of usability test.
2. To make sure a new or redesigned Web site solves the problems it was intended to address and does not introduce new problems. This type of test is known as a *validation* test. A validation test requires that the Web site meet specified benchmarks or standards, such as maximum time to find a piece of information or minimum number of correct answers.
3. To compare two or more Web sites or design approaches. This type of usability test is known as a *comparative* usability test. Comparative usability tests are done at the beginning of a Web redesign project (to compare two different design approaches) or after a redesign project has been completed (to compare the current design to the new design to make sure the new design is more usable than the old). In the latter case, the comparative usability test is being used as a type of validation test.

A fourth type of usability test, the *exploratory* test (Rubin, 1994), is used to determine users' mental map of the domain for which an application is being designed. Exploratory tests have less applicability to Web sites and will not be discussed here.

Identify the User Tasks to Be Tested

The heart of usability testing is the tasks or questions users are asked to perform on the Web site. It is important that the questions be representative of typical user tasks—the things users seek to accomplish when they come to the Web site. The temptation to test tasks the institution wants to promote should be resisted. The test task "Find how to donate to the library" may be completed by 100 percent of the testers (assuming a prominent link on the home page); however, this does not ensure that the Web site is usable if that is not the reason users come to the Web site. There are several ways to find what user tasks to test:

1. Consult with key stakeholders for the Web site, such as public services staff and faculty. This step can help build stakeholder buy-in and acceptance of the test results. Getting their help setting the direction of the testing at the beginning can be invaluable later on.
2. Get information from users via surveys or focus groups or by consulting log files, to determine what users use the Web site for and what is important to them in it.

Once the list of typical user tasks—the reason they come to the Web site—has been created, the tasks need to be converted to specific tasks or questions for usability testing (Figure 7.1).

Number of Usability Test Tasks

The number of tasks to include in a usability test is determined by the time available for the test. If usability testing is being done with walk-in volunteers, 30 minutes may be about the maximum amount of time one can expect people to contribute. If tests have been scheduled ahead of time, longer tests are possible. Pretesting the usability test with two or three people who are

55

Figure 7.1: Typical User Tasks Conversion for Testing	
Typical user tasks	Test questions or tasks
Find if the library has a particular book	"Does the library have *Long Way Gone: Memoirs of a Boy Soldier*, by Ishmael Beah?
Find articles on a topic	"Find three articles on rural efforts to spread awareness of AIDS prevention methods in Africa."
Find if the library has access to a particular journal	"Does the library have access to the article 'The effectiveness of inhibitors in human predictive judgments depends on the strength of the positive predictor,' published in the journal *Learning & Behavior*?"
Find the hours the library is open	"What time does the Chemistry Library close on Friday, April 27, 2007?"

typical users will ensure the tasks are clearly worded and can be accomplished, and also provide information on the length of time required for the test.

User Groups

If the library Web site has different user groups, different tasks may be required. For example, accessing electronic reserves readings might be an appropriate task for undergraduates, while finding the form to add readings to electronic reserves might be a more suitable task for a faculty member.

Prepare a Script

A script should be prepared covering what the test moderator will say, including the welcome, how the test will be conducted, and the tasks. Having a script ensures consistency from test to test and between test moderators. Having written copies of the tasks for the participants, as well as any additional observers and recorders, helps keep everyone together during the test.

Recording Data

Some thought should be given to what data is to be gathered during the usability test and how it will be captured; this will determine in large part the design of the test. One should capture the information needed to facilitate decision making. Other considerations include how the results of the testing will be communicated and what information will be needed in the future if iterative testing is to be done.

Possible types of data to capture:

1. *Success rate:* Were users able to find the information using the Web site?
2. *Time:* How long did it take users to find the information? This is particularly useful for before-and-after comparisons, as well as for validation testing.
3. *Path:* How did users get to the information—the links clicked, method used (browse or search)? Did they use the optimal path or not?
4. *User comments:* This is qualitative information, as opposed to the quantitative information (success rate, time, etc.). Encouraging test participants to "talk aloud" about what they are thinking during the test is one way to gather this information; post-test debriefing is another. Video recordings of users' expressions can be revealing. Seeing an undergraduate's blank stare can go a long way towards convincing stakeholders of problems with a favorite page.

Once the information to be recorded has been determined, provision will need to be made to capture it for later analysis and sharing. In most cases, having a recorder who can act as an additional observer, as well as take notes or fill out forms, is very useful. Even if other recording techniques are being used, one should take notes that could substitute for the recording device should it fail, and also provide additional insights. An increasingly popular usability test recording method is screen capture software (Morae, Camtasia, Hypercam, etc.). This software records the users' mouse movements and pages visited. One of the benefits of user testing is to see users using the Web site in totally unexpected ways. Screen captures and particularly video can help capture and convey this to others not present at the test sessions. Audio recording, with video or separately, can help record user comments. Video recording of users' expressions can convey dramatically the impact of users' problems with the Web site, but raises privacy considerations and may require signed release forms.

Forms and Scoring

For most usability tests, forms can greatly facilitate the process of recording and analyzing test data. Forms are particularly well suited to gathering demographic data, the date, and the moderator. They can also include the questions with areas to record:

1. Time. Recording how long it took users to find the information can help compare alternative designs.
2. The number of clicks, recording the path through the site. Did the test participant find the most direct path to the information? Did participants consistently use a less efficient means to get to the information? Recording the path, the series of links clicked, and the searches entered can help capture this information for subsequent analysis.
3. A scoring of the results. A three point-scale might be used to rate how the participant did on each question. For example:
    i. The question was answered or task completed on the first attempt.
    ii. The participant failed to find it the first time, tried a different approach and found the information on a second or subsequent attempt.
    iii. The information was not found.

These scores can be useful in comparing how different user populations did before and after the redesign.

Pretest the Test

It is easy to overlook this step, particularly if the test is brief and limited in scope. Pretesting can identify problems with the questions, recording methodology, or test design. It is frustrating to realize that a test is not capturing the data required to answer the question being asked. Pretesting can prevent this from happening. In addition, pretests give moderators and recorders practice, allowing them to get more comfortable in their roles.

Logistics

Determine where and how the usability tests will be administered. Test locations can vary from a table set up in a public area, to a separate room in the library, to going to the office of the test participant.

Getting Participants

How many participants will be needed? The traditional answer, based on Nielsen (2000), is 5–8. If there are distinct user groups, several representatives from each should be tested. Care should be taken to obtain representative test participants. Student workers who have spent three years working in reference might not be the best choice for testing the library catalog.

Conducting the Usability Test

When conducting a usability test, there are a number of things you can do to set the test participant at ease and explain the what, why, and how of the usability test.

1. Welcome the participant.
2. Introduce yourself and the recorder.
3. Explain why the test is being conducted and what you hope to learn.
4. Gather any demographic data you need.
5. If your institution has an institutional review board (IRB), and the testing requires approval, have the participant sign the form.
6. Explain how the test will be conducted. For example, you will be reading the questions and the recorder will be noting comments.
7. Convey the message "We're not testing you, you're helping us test the site."
8. Ask if they have any questions before you begin.

Tips for Effective Moderation

- Encourage the test participant to talk out loud. Explain that doing so will help you understand better what the participant is thinking.
- If the participant is having problems with a task, have them move on after a minute or so. Tell them that they've given you useful information about the feature being tested.
- Read questions out loud or have the test participant read them out loud to ensure comprehension. Have a written copy for the test participant to refer to.

- Do not answer questions or give hints to the test participant. It may be painful to watch a participant struggle; however, a usability test is not the setting in which to do bibliographic instruction. Any tips or coaching will contaminate the results. Answer any questions the participant may have after the test.
- If you are comparing two alternative design approaches and are testing all participants on both, start half the participants on one version and half on the other to avoid test order bias.
- If you are doing validation testing (comparing an existing design to a redesign of the site) test half on the original site only, half on the redesigned site only, then compare results.
- At the end of the test, debrief the participants. If you are comparing alternative designs, ask which they liked better and why. Ask for comments or suggestions. Questions such as "What three things could we do to make the Web site better?" can elicit potentially useful comments. A brief survey can be a tool for gathering information about alternate designs ("Rate each design on a scale of 1-5 on the following criteria"). End by asking the participant if they have any questions or if they have anything else they'd like to tell you. Thank them and give them any incentive promised for participating in the testing.

After the Test Participant Leaves

After the test participant has left, debrief with the recorder. Write up a brief summary of the test with your impressions and the significant findings while they are still fresh in your mind.

Analyzing the Results

1. Gather the data from all the tests and compile it into a single document; spreadsheets work well for this.
2. Provide numerical summaries ("82 percent of graduate students correctly answered question 4, while only 71 percent of undergraduates found the answer.")
3. Write up a narrative description of what you think the findings mean.
4. If you've done screen or video captures, edit to enable presentation of key findings.

Unless you are the Webmaster, you need to document and convey the results to stakeholders and those responsible for Web site design and maintenance. Consider how you will keep the documentation for later reference. Make it available on a Web site if possible. Having a record of the test results allows you to compare the usability of the site over time as changes are made.

Conclusion

Usability testing is the most powerful usability method for identifying problems users have using the library's Web site to accomplish their tasks. Usability testing is a good way to compare alternative Web design approaches, and to validate a new Web design—making sure it works as expected and does not introduce new usability problems.

Usability testing should not be the only technique you use to evaluate a Web site, but if you only have the time or resources available for one usability technique, it should be usability testing. Usability testing can provide useful insights when used in its most basic form; the benefits increase as usability testing is done more thoroughly, iteratively, and in conjunction with other Web site assessment techniques.

References

Battleson, Brenda, Austin Booth, and Jane Weintrop. 2001. "Usability Testing of an Academic Library Web Site: A Case Study," *Journal of Academic Librarianship*, 27, no. 3 (May): 188–198.

Covey, Denise T. 2002. "Usage and Usability Assessment: Library Practices and Concerns." Washington, DC: Digital Library Federation and Council on Library and Information Resources.

Kirkwood, Harold. 2007. "Usability Case Study: Purdue University Libraries." In *Making Library Web Sites Usable: A LITA Guide*. New York: Neal-Schuman.

Nielsen, Jakob. 2000. "Why You Only Need to Test with 5 Users." Alertbox (March 19.) Available: www.useit.com/alertbox/20000319.html

Nielsen, Jakob. 2003. "Usability 101: Introduction to Usability." Alertbox (August 25). Available: www.useit.com/alertbox/20030825.html

Rubin, Jeffrey. 1994. *Handbook of Usability Testing*. New York: Wiley.

University of Washington Libraries. 2005. "Guide to Planning and Conducting Usability Tests." Available: www.lib.washington.edu/usability/guidelines/usability-guidelines.htm

Chapter 8

Web Server Logs Analysis

Michelle Dalmau
and Juliet L. Hardesty

Introduction

Libraries have a strong tradition of relying on transaction logs to determine usage patterns for catalogs and other electronic resources such as databases and serials (Tolle, 1983; Sullenger, 1997; Blecic et al., 1998; Covey, 2002; Ghaphery, 2005; Gauger and Kacena, 2006).[1] Gathering log data is a function handled by servers. The captured data can be automatically parsed by statistical software such as the open-source solutions Webalizer (www.mrunix.net/Webalizer/) or AWStats (http://awstats.sourceforge.net) to support visualizations of the data commonly collected by server-side transaction logs: Page hits, referrers, browser, and so on. Low-overhead, low-cost solutions provided by capturing and processing log data and straightforward reporting provided by software packages are just two reasons library professionals have historically adopted logs analysis as a way to gauge user experience. More importantly, libraries have always championed automation and technology, and as technological innovators, library professionals naturally gravitated to logs analysis as a form of user assessment. As libraries continue to develop and implement information retrieval systems such as digital libraries and portal Web sites, which increasingly support more complex user interactions, they contribute to the evolving landscape of logs analysis as an activity that requires more rigorous adaptation beyond the default reports provided by the commonly used statistical software tools.

Unlike other usability techniques that focus on direct contact with small, select groups of users, server logs provide inexpensive and unobtrusive

61

---

1. For an overview of transaction logs analysis conducted in libraries, see T. A. Peters' 1993 article, "The History and Development of Transaction Logs Analysis," published in *Library Hi Tech*.

insight to a greater audience (Jansen, 2006). The scope of analysis can range from following a single user's visit to examining data recorded over many months to find the most popular search terms or information resources. Likewise, as in heuristic evaluation, server logs can help uncover existing problems or roadblocks that prevent the efficient or effective use of an online resource. If server logs show that users are continually searching on terms that generate no results or that the most popular page is one that is not updated, it may be concluded that users are not having an optimal experience with the electronic resource, and steps can be taken to correct the situation. Server logs alone cannot tell the full story, however. Without knowing why users take the actions they take—without surveying and interviewing users—there is no way to know for certain whether or not the paths recorded in the server logs or the statistics calculated indicate a real problem (Jansen, 2006; Covey, 2002). As library electronic resources become more interactive, logs serve as a tool that can validate findings from more subjective usability methods such as interviews, surveys, and task-based analysis.

Traditionally, server administrators have relied on log data to monitor levels of traffic and error reports to ensure optimal performance of a system. Today this is still the case, but usability practitioners in libraries are parsing log data in more meaningful ways to help inform the design of new online resources and enhance existing resources.

Advantages and Disadvantages of Transaction Logs Analysis

Denise Troll Covey's comprehensive publication *Usage and Usability Assessment: Library Practices and Concerns* details a series of weaknesses attributed to logs analysis followed by reasons to conduct transaction logs analysis despite these weaknesses: "identify user communities; identify patterns of use; project future needs for services and collections; assess user satisfaction; inform digital collection development decisions," and so on (2002, section 3.2). Creative and rigorous logs analysis can shed light on many of the goals Covey identifies, but not always in a comprehensive manner. Logs analysis can only tell us what the user is doing, not why. However, logs analysis can provide usability practitioners with a foundation for developing improvements and enhancements, and when combined with other user studies can provide insight into the user experience.

As with all usability methods, logs analysis comes with its own set of strengths and weaknesses. Understanding these will enable the usability practitioner to plan better his/her approach to analysis and how the results can be used to inform improvements.

Advantages

One of the key advantages of gathering log data is its unobtrusive nature; it does not require imposing on a user's time to collect feedback. Furthermore, if you are affiliated with an institution governed by an institutional review board (IRB) and you intend to publish the findings from a logs study, you may not be required to file for human subjects approval so long as personally identifying information such as e-mail addresses and, in some cases, IP numbers are removed from the data set. Data collection is automatic and requires little or no intervention by the usability practitioner. This is especially important because of the comprehensive nature of log data: It reflects the entire user population and can be systematically processed to reveal usage patterns. Log data is considered objective, "real" data, not subject to common biases associated with self-reporting methods. As quantifiable data, it is easily analyzed using spreadsheets and databases, not to mention out-of-box statistical software.

Disadvantages

Analysis of log data can be time consuming, and not all data is straightforward, especially user queries, as these may require additional interpretation governed by content guidelines for consistent treatment. Data also needs to be pre-filtered to ensure analysis is performed against actual usage. Search engine spiders, which account for a large number of entries in a typical log file, can distort findings by inflating log entries. It is also important to keep in mind that data is inherently biased by the constraints of the interface and functionality; therefore, assessment needs to take into consideration the limitations or restrictions of an interface by reconciling, discarding, or contextualizing data in light of these constraints. Because user context and motivations are unknown, information needs are not clear. Therefore, problems encountered with the interface are only revealed by system responses, not user responses. Yet another weakness is that data capture is usually session-based, making it difficult to track usage and discovery patterns over time. This makes the data difficult to generalize as it captures only a particular moment of a user's experience.

Alternatives to Transaction Logs Analysis

While out-of-box statistical software packages provide a good overview of usage, too often they do not enable libraries to uncover more fundamental usage patterns that can serve both to validate certain features of online resources and expose weaknesses of these resources. Usability practitioners in libraries are more commonly adopting a "deep log analysis" approach, as championed by David Nicholas and colleagues (Nicholas et al., 2006; Nicholas, Huntington

63

and Watkinson, 2005). According to Nicholas et al. (2005: 251), deep log analysis is a multistep process:

> Firstly, the assumptions on how the data are defined and recorded (for instance, who is a user, what is a hit, etc.) are questioned and realigned as necessary, and their statistical significance assessed. This is important, as skewed data is a real problem. This ensures that incorrect, overinflated readings that give a false sense of achievement/progress are avoided. Secondly, the raw data are re-engineered to provide more powerful metrics and to ensure that data gathering is better aligned to organizational goals. The third step is to enrich the usage data by adding user demographic data (e.g., occupation, subject specialist), either with data obtained from a subscriber database (ideal) or online questionnaires (not so ideal, as user data cannot be mapped so closely on usage data).

Various methods can be adopted to satisfy the "deep log analysis" approach. They range from customizing log scripts to go beyond the gathering of standard server-side transactions to multifaceted user study approaches that better contextualize standard log data. The former method may be achieved using tools like Log4j (http://logging.apache.org/log4j/docs/), an open source logging application developed under the Apache Jakarta project for more robust logging of Java-based applications. This package is able to capture user-specified criteria from various points of user interaction within an application such as files, databases, and GUI components (Chauhan, 2003). The Indiana University Digital Library Program (IUDLP) uses Log4j for specialized logging of many of its digital library collections. In particular, the IUDLP adapted this tool for capturing the user's discovery patterns by recording the exact formation of user queries submitted in simple and advanced search pages, including fields and filters chosen, and by recording links clicked in browse and results pages. Formatting log data using Log4j makes it easier to parse and therefore understand how users combine categories provided in a faceted browse of an IUDLP collection. The following are sample log data from Log4j:

> 2004-04-04 19:22:04 [BROWSE] state:"Illinois" AND year:"1966" AND genre:"Portraits"
> 2004-04-11 23:08:22 [BROWSE] state:"California" AND city:"San Francisco" AND subject:"Marine terminals"

The data captured by Log4j not only reveals the type of searches users are conducting, but also allows for the comparison of discovery modes and preferred discovery interactions.

Multifaceted approaches to user studies that include logs analysis are increasingly commonplace in libraries. Fran Diamond notes in her 2003 article, "Web Traffic Analytics and User Experience,"

We information architects and user experience folks tend to prefer dealing with the real users, the designs, and the creative expression of ideas, and not so much with the numbers. We spend our time developing prototypes, testing designs with users, and then interpreting those results for a creative solution that provides outstanding user experiences. . . . By looking at the data on what users do on the site, however, you can enhance your effectiveness as a [user] specialist. You already have information and knowledge gained through observation and direct questioning of individual users. Now, you can add to that insights gained from the broad swath of information pulled during their actions on the site (para. 1).

Usability practitioners in libraries often combine qualitative methods associated with social science research such as observations, interviews, and surveys with log data to arrive at a user-centric understanding of the use of online library resources (Assadi et al., 2003; Jones et al., 2004). Inherent weaknesses of assessing log data alone can be overcome by using various user-centered techniques. The Indiana University Libraries have successfully adopted both approaches (customized logs and combination user studies) to improve their library online resources, as seen in the case study described below.

Case Study: Indiana University Libraries

Indiana University Bloomington Libraries Web Site

On a regular basis, the Indiana University Bloomington (IUB) Libraries Web site (www.libraries.iub.edu) solicits feedback from users via e-mail, reference interviews (both online and in-person), and server log analysis. The Web site uses several log analysis and statistical software packages including Analog (www.analog.cx), AWStats, Webalizer, and ReportMagic (www.report-magic.org). All these packages provide the usual referral, request, and redirect reports along with browser-type breakdowns and traffic statistics. For the most part, these software packages provide different views of the same information. Since it can be helpful to see the same data represented differently, all these statistical software packages are made available to library staff who manage content on the IUB Libraries Web site.

The IUB Libraries also have implemented customized logging, which tracks searches through a single user session, as well as overall library Web site page visits, online library resource use, and search terms. Similar information can be gleaned from the packaged software, but the difficulties inherent in using a software package meant to harness all information from a Web server can make this software difficult to use, as Covey (2002) describes:

Despite the level of creative analysis and application of Web usage data at some institutions, even these libraries are not happy with the software they use to analyze Web logs. The logs are huge and analysis is cumbersome, sometimes exceeding the capacity of the software. Libraries are simultaneously looking for alternative software and trying to figure out what data are useful to track, how to gather and analyze the data efficiently, and how to present the data appropriately to inform decisions (Ch. 3, Sec. 5).

Custom logging on the IUB Libraries Web site was created using PHP with a MySQL database. The entire Web site is database-driven, allowing page owners (library staff responsible for the content of library Web site pages), subject area advocates (library staff responsible for defining subject areas for online library resources available through the Web site), and electronic resource advocates (library staff responsible for online library resources) to update content by updating the database. This method of constructing the Web site also allows Web pages and electronic resources accessed to be counted. All Web pages and electronic resources stored in the database have a counter field. Each time a Web page or electronic resource is accessed by a user, the count is increased by one. The reports that show the results of this logging can use the counts to show information such as which resources are accessed the most through the library Web site, which subject areas are accessed the most through the library Web site, and which library Web site pages receive the most visits.

The custom logging developed for the IUB Libraries Web site serves to improve the usability of the Web site on an ongoing basis. Web page owners can view reports from these logs at any time and get a sense of how users navigate, their destination points, the kinds of content they are looking for, and how this information could affect the content of those managed pages. Examples of these reports include monthly page hits for each page of the Web site, including defined subsets like subject pages for easier evaluation, and the top 100 searches entered in the search engine on the database search page. These statistics can help page owners better manage their respective content areas. For example, if a spike is noticed in the number of times the graduate carrels page is accessed, that page's owner can take that information as a signal to ensure the carrels page accurately reflects the information required to reserve a carrel.

Resource and subject advocates, charged with making decisions about which online resources to offer through the Web site, what information to provide about those resources, and which resources to associate with which subjects, also find the customized search logging helpful. Each time a search is conducted, it is aggregated in a master list of search terms. Figure 8.1 shows an IUB Libraries Web Site "Find Information" Search terms report. The first 10 of the top 100 search terms entered by users in the "Find Information" search engine are shown here. This report reflects the count since the Web site went live in 2002.

Figure 8.1: IUB Libraries Search Terms Report	
Keyword Search Terms	Count
1 | jstor	5438
2 | rlin	3274
3 | wall street journal	2574
4 | new york times	2229
5 | Nature	1818
6 | science	1567
7 | nyt	1352
8 | Harvard Business Review	1318
9 | dissertation abstracts	1119
10 | Biological Abstracts	1108

If a user accesses an electronic resource, a counter associated with that re-source is incremented (similar to the "click throughs" method described by Covey, 2002). Likewise, if a subject page is accessed, a log tracks the number of times that subject page is viewed, giving an indication of the paths users are taking to learn about or access electronic resources offered through the Web site. In this sense, the resource and subject advocates become the usability practitioners with the aid of these log tools, using search terms from real users to enhance the list of search terms for a resource and guide users to appropriate resources on the library Web site, as well as to the subjects used to describe and categorize the resources.

The error-recording system on the IUB Libraries Web site provides another example of customized logging. If a page owner includes a link to another page within the Web site and the target page is unavailable, the next time that link is clicked, a page link error is recorded. In addition, the owner of the page containing the erroneous link is notified via e-mail of the problem link on that page. These error logs are always available for review, and they assist content managers, who are most likely responsible for a wide range of pages, in keeping content current and accurate.

The server logs also have become an important tool in the implementation of the Google Search Appliance (www.google.com/appliance) for searching the

IUB Libraries Web site. Just as the customized search reports help page owners and resource advocates manage the content on the site, they also help construct such specialized areas of the Google Search Appliance as Keyword Matches, designed to provide the single most likely match to the user's term in a highlighted initial position in the search results (similar to the "Sponsored Links" in Google.com). By taking the top set of search terms submitted to the libraries' Web site from the customized search log (as can be seen in Figure 8.1), keyword matches can be mapped to the most popular resources and services, making the user's path to that resource or service more immediate and prominent.

Customized search term logging also can help decide what metadata should appear on the search results page. Search results from the Google Search Appliance can show page metadata as it is entered by the page owner. Author, keywords, and description for a page can be displayed along with the page title and URL, providing the user with additional information for deciding whether or not a search result is relevant. Log data containing search terms is useful in determining if there are terms that need to be highlighted as keyword matches in search results for common queries.

Stemming, or applying searches to variations of the entered search term, also can be customized in the Google Search Appliance. Log data from search terms entered by users has proven helpful here as well. Search terms can be mapped to authoritative terms ("ereserves" can be expanded to search "electronic reserves") or acronyms ("council on library and information resources" can be mapped to "clir"). Users are then prompted to expand their search and are given feedback on what the search engine is doing with their search terms. The search term logs tracked by the IUB Libraries Web site provide guides for developing additional useful mappings. If logs show users are searching for "undergraduate library," then stemming can be applied in the Google Search Appliance to map that search term to "Wells Library" (the name of the building that houses this library), as well as "Information Commons" (the other name by which this library/area of the building is known).

The IUB Libraries offer the traditional prepackaged views of Web server logs while also making active use of the information being logged about user searches and actions to constantly improve the service provided by the libraries' Web site, as in the case of mapping search terms to authoritative terms to ensure hits, or amassing a set of key matches to improve retrieval. Combining out-of-box and custom log solutions supports the kinds of data analysis suited for both gradual and rapid enhancements of the IUB Libraries' Web site.

Indiana University Digital Library Program

The Indiana University Digital Library Program (IUDLP) applied its own flavor of "deep log analysis" with the IN Harmony: Sheet Music from Indiana project (IN Harmony) (www.dlib.indiana.edu/projects/inharmony/), a collaboration between Indiana University, Indiana State Library, Indiana State Museum, and Indiana Historical Society. IN Harmony is funded by an Institute of Museum and Library Services National Leadership Grant, and aims to establish a standards-based shared cataloging tool for describing sheet music and to provide online access to approximately 10,000 pieces of Indiana-related sheet music. To successfully meet these goals, the project is committed to iterative usability testing and has, to date, completed three user studies: Query Logs Analysis Study (www.dlib.indiana.edu/projects/inharmony/projectDoc/usability/logs/index.shtml), Card Sort and Task Scenario Study (www.dlib.indiana.edu/projects/inharmony/projectDoc/usability/cardSortTasks/index.shtml), and Reference Email Content Analysis Study (www.dlib.indiana.edu/projects/inharmony/projectDoc/usability/email/index.shtml).

The first in a series of user studies, conducted primarily to inform the design of the metadata model and sheet music cataloging tool for IN Harmony, was a logs study (Query Logs Analysis Study). This study assessed actual user queries and discovery patterns extracted from server logs generated by two online sheet music Web sites: The Sheet Music Consortium (SMC) (http://digital.library.ucla.edu/sheetmusic/), a collection comprised of heterogeneous metadata brought together via the Open Archives Initiative Protocol for Metadata Harvesting (OAI-PMH) using unqualified Dublin Core, and the Indiana University Sheet Music Collection (IUSM) (www.dlib.indiana.edu/collections/sheetmusic/), a collection comprised of homogenous metadata based on custom database fields. The purpose of the logs study was to understand:

- relative use of browse, search, and advanced search options
- frequency of known-item (specific) versus unknown-item (general) searching
  - types of known-item searches conducted (title, name, etc.)
  - types of unknown-item searches conducted (topical, genre, etc.)

The study analyzed a 10 percent random sample of log data consisting of timestamps, types of searches (browse, search, advanced search), queries, fields selected (keyword, title, etc.) and Boolean and other advanced operators entered. The original log data was processed and collected according to a set of predefined parsing rules from both Web sites during a six-month period in 2004; the derived 10 percent sample included 2,542 log entries. The sample, generated to facilitate the additional level of qualitative analysis of the queries required for this study, was taken after entries by search engine spiders had been filtered from the data. The log data was formatted in a comma delimited format (CSV) using Perl scripts for easy import into spreadsheets or databases.

69

Figure 8.2: Number of Log Entries, June–November 2004						
2004	ORIGINAL		FILTERED		SAMPLE	
	IUSM	SMC	IUSM	SMC	IUSM	SMC
June	2,552	1,625	1,558	1,618	155	162
July	55,573	1,665	1765	1,665	176	166
August	11,315	1,630	1,214	1,620	120	162
September	3,846	3,613	1,883	3,613	188	361
October	5,055	2,906	3,669	2,900	365	290
November	1,710	2,853	1,127	2,851	112	285
TOTAL	80,051	14,292	11,216	14,267	1,116	2,536

Figure 8.2 shows the total number of log entries harvested in a six-month period in 2004 from Indiana University Sheet Music Collection (IUSM) and the Sheet Music Consortium (SMC), followed by the number after filtering for search engine spiders, followed by the final sample of log entries analyzed. The spike in the July data for IUSM reveals the inflated entries generated by search engine spiders.

The data was then analyzed using an Excel spreadsheet with macros and advanced filtering options to determine the number of:

- browse, search, and advanced searches
- user-specified queries of keyword, subject, names/composer, and so on
  - mappings of keyword searches to specific fields
  - mappings of subject searches to subject sub-categories (topical, form, genre, style, temporal, geographic, etc.)
  - known-item versus unknown-item queries
  - year searches

Additional search inputs were also analyzed, including desired content (e.g., lyrics versus sheet music), syntax/operators used, and advanced search fields selected. To ensure accurate and consistent interpretation of the data, a small subset of the data was subjected to content analysis. Guidelines were written to govern the interpretation of queries and the subsequent mapping to pre-defined and user-defined search fields, such as title, subject, genre, etc. The coding guidelines were primarily straightforward (e.g., a definition of "title" with examples), but some areas of analysis were more intricate, especially in the case of subject-related queries.[2] The content analysis underwent two passes: First by the usability practitioner, then by a metadata and music domain expert.

The findings revealed a great deal of basic yet useful information. For instance, the team learned that most people conduct known-item searching when looking for sheet music: Name (23 percent and 28 percent) and title (19 percent and 12 percent) for IUSM and SMC respectively. Subject-specified searches (e.g., users searching in a subject field) are few (IUSM and SMC, <3 percent); however, a significant number of subject keyword searches were conducted (19 percent, n=1,695). Most users conducted keyword searches (IUSM 54 percent, SMC 65 percent). Those that conducted advanced searches (IUSM 20 percent, SMC 12 percent) almost always left the default fields selected. Both the IUSM and SMC logs reveal that most of the advanced searches conducted were actually simple keyword searches. User error, defined by misspellings, incorrect use of operators/syntax, and so on, contributed to only a small percentage of queries resulting in no hits. (To see complete documentation of the logs analysis findings including charts and graphs, see www.dlib.indiana.edu/projects/inharmony/projectDoc/usability/logs/final Report_INHarmonyLogsAnalysis.pdf) Most of the no-hits were caused by users looking for sheet music not represented in the collection. More importantly, as with subject-related searches, the team also was able to uncover patterns that were more meaningful. The queries revealed that users of sheet music have a multifaceted conception of "subject;" they searched for genres, styles of music, and instrumentation, as well as topical subjects. Rather than lump all these access points under the generic "subject," the more specific facets formed the basis of key access points to be represented in the metadata model. [3] Table 8.3 lists the researcher-assigned subject-related categories that emerged from the mapping of subject-related queries harvested from the logs.

71

2. We have learned from the literature and our own findings that users of sheet music have unique discovery needs especially in subject access. Existing research in this area has confirmed that users do not approach subject access in a uniform or predictable way; subject searches typically include topic, form, genre, style, and geographic terms, thereby potentially complicating access. To learn more about how our subject analysis of the log data impacted the IN Harmony metadata model and cataloging tool, see "The IN Harmony Project: Developing a Flexible Metadata Model for the Description and Discovery of Sheet Music" by Jenn Riley and Michelle Dalmau in *The Electronic Library*, volume 25, number 2 (2007).

3. To test our own categorical constructs derived from subject-terms analysis, we conducted a card sort study composed of 50 recurring concepts harvested from the log entries. Participants were asked to group these concepts and create categories. To learn more about how the findings from the logs study informed the card sort study and the outcomes of that study, see: www.dlib.indiana.edu/projects/inharmony/projectDoc/usability/cardSortTasks/index.shtml

Figure 8.3: Subject Categories and Number of Searches								
Researcher Assigned Subject Categories	IUSM # of Subject-Specified Searches		SMC # of Subject-Specified Searches		IUSM # of Subject-Keyword Searches		SMC # of Subject-Keyword Searches	
Genre/Form/Style	20	27%	25	76%	95	54%	72	47%
Instrumentation	10	14%	2	6%	40	23%	49	32%
Topic	24	32%	1	3%	27	16%	15	10%
Geographic	2	3%	1	3%	6	3%	11	7%
Language	0	0%	0	0%	1	1%	4	3%
Presentation Form	0	0%	2	6%	4	2%	2	1%
Medium	0	0%	0	0%	1	1%	0	0%
Temporal	0	0%	1	3%	0	0%	0	0%
Unknown	2	3%	0	0%	0	0%	0	0%
Non-Subject Terms	16	21%	1	3%	0	0%	0	0%
Total	74	100%	33	100%	174	100%	153	100%

A total of 19 percent of (keyword and user-specified) searches were typed as "subject." These research-assigned subject categories were later corroborated by the findings of the card sort study, second in the series of user studies.

The logs analysis findings have answered many questions, but also generated many more: Are users looking for musical content or cover art? Does the user distinguish between genre, form, and style? Are the infrequently occurring yet unique queries like sheet music plate numbers essential for discovery by certain types of sheet music users? Despite the issues raised by the logs study, the hybrid quantitative and qualitative approach resulted in findings that formed the foundation for the metadata model and cataloging tool. For instance, because title and names are the most common searches, various access points were created for title (proper title, alternative title, first line of chorus, etc.), and names were entered in an authoritative fashion to improve retrieval. Questions that arose as a result of the logs study, primarily those related to subject-related access and the categories and metadata fields derived by the researchers, formed the basis of subsequent user studies. The log study and subsequent studies that built upon the actual log data and the findings from the analysis of that log data led to a modular metadata model that meets the diverse cataloging needs of the IN Harmony partners, as well as the diverse discovery needs of the users.

Conclusion

Both the IUB Libraries Web site and the IN Harmony project utilized log data to inform not only interface requirements, but metadata requirements as well. Metadata can make or break the interface. Fortunately, certain usability methods such as logs analysis and card sorts are particularly well suited for uncovering metadata-related issues, whether they relate to improved retrieval or more intuitive navigation and exploration of an online resource. In addition to tracking metadata issues using log data, both the IUB Libraries Web site and IN Harmony project have derived information from the log entries to ensure that functionality provided by both resources results in the desired user experience.

The Indiana University Libraries are currently reassessing their log capture process to ensure a more consistent, robust gathering of log data for analysis. Several improvements will be undertaken to meet this need. For the IUB Libraries, defining better relationships among log data collected is in the forefront; for instance, associating the number of times a resource is accessed with the page from which that resource was accessed. This connection will help page owners and subject and resource advocates alike know more accurately how users are accessing resources from the IUB Libraries Web site. Subject page counts, electronic resource counts, and search terms can all give good indications of the most likely paths being taken, but tying this information together in the logs and reports will help the IUB Libraries know what paths are the most critical to users finding resources within the Web site. For the Indiana University Digital Library Program, standardizing log capture across similar collections and log terminology for comparing usage patterns across collections is necessary, especially in light of the new infrastructure work under development.[4] The common terminology will contribute to more uniform, universally understood reporting of log data, as well as provide points from which to compare or contrast similar or even dissimilar digital library resources.

Successful logs analysis, whether or not a "deep analysis" approach is employed, requires clearly defined goals based on the users' needs and experiences. Once goals are stated, deriving metrics and strategies for processing the

73

---

4. The IUDLP is implementing FEDORA as their infrastructure for digital object repository. See the Fedora Web site for more information: www.fedora.info/

data will come more naturally. For "deep analysis," the time spent in defining precise parsing and content analysis rules for creative "views" of the log entries, and guidelines for qualitative analysis will facilitate a smoother, more consistent data analysis process.

When questions arise, the building-block approach to user studies is one way to formulate answers. Questions should be factored into subsequent user studies. Data gathered from the logs may be used as a point of reference when learning more from users. Combining and integrating logs analysis with other user studies will provide the context required for a solid set of functional requirements and enhancements.

Logs generate volumes of data, but with planning and foresight, mining them will certainly help improve online library resources.

References

Assadi, Houssem, Thomas Beauvisage, Catherine Lupovici, and Thierry Cloarec. 2003. "Users and Uses of Online Digital Libraries in France." In *Research and Advanced Technology for Digital Libraries* (1–12). Berlin: Springer.

Blecic, Deborah D., Nirmala S. Bangalore, Josephine L. Dorsch, Cynthia L. Henderson, Melissa H. Koenig, and Ann C. Weller. 1998. "Using Transaction Log Analysis to Improve OPAC Retrieval Results." *College & Research Libraries* 59, no. 1: 39–50.

Chauhan, Mugdha. 2003. "Logging with Log4j: An Efficient Way to Log Java Applications." Available: www.developer.com/open/article.php/3097221 (accessed October 19, 2007)

Covey, Denise Troll. 2002. *Usage and Usability Assessment: Library Practices and Concerns.* Washington, DC: Council on Library and Information Resources.

Diamond, Fran. 2003. "Web Traffic Analytics and User Experience." Available: www.boxesandarrows.com/view/Web_traffic_analytics_and_user_experience (accessed October 19, 2007)

Gauger, Barbara, and Carolyn Kacena. 2006. "JSTOR Usage Data and What It Can Tell Us about Ourselves: Is There Predictability Based on Historical Use by Libraries of Similar Size?" *OCLC Systems & Services* 22, no. 1: 43–55.

Ghaphery, Jimmy. 2005. "Too quick? Log Analysis of Quick Links from an Academic Library Web Site." *OCLC Systems & Services* 21, no. 3: 148–155.

Jansen, Bernard J. 2006. "Search Log Analysis: What It Is, What's Been Done, How To Do It." *Library & Information Science Research* 28, no. 3: 407–432.

Jones, C., S. Giersch, T. Sumner, M. Wright, A. Coleman, and L. Bartolo. 2004. "Developing a Web Analytics Strategy for the National Science Digital Library." *D-Lib Magazine*, 10. Available; www.dlib.org/dlib/october04/coleman/10coleman. html (accessed October 19, 2007)

Nicholas, David, Paul Huntington, Hamid R. Jamali, and Carol Tenopir. 2006. "What Deep Log Analysis Tells Us about the Impact of Big Deals: Case Study Ohio-Link." *Journal of Documentation* 62, no. 4: 482–508.

Nicholas, David, Paul Huntington, and Anthony Watkinson. 2005. "Scholarly Journal Usage: The Results of Deep Log Analysis." *Journal of Documentation* 61, no. 2: 248–280.

Sullenger, P. 1997. "A Serials Transaction Log Analysis." *Serials Review* 23, no. 3: 21–26.

Tolle, John E. 1983. "Transaction Log Analysis: Online Catalogs." In *Research and Development in Information Retrieval, Sixth Annual International ACM SIGIR Conference*, ed. J. Kuehn (147–160). Baltimore, MD: ACM.

Chapter 9

Attracting Users for Testing
Michael Yunkin

Introduction

Usability testing cannot begin without test participants, but recruiting them often takes a lot of work and creativity. In an academic setting, some may assume it is easy to find volunteers; after all, we deal with students every day. In practice, however, it's just not that easy. Students are busy, often difficult to contact, and not always reliable. Successful recruitment too often means "making it worth their while"—not an easy thing to do on a limited or nonexistent budget. To overcome the obstacles inherent in recruiting test participants, a well-defined recruitment strategy is a necessity.

Institutional Review Boards and Recruitment

Defining and carrying out a recruitment strategy is not just good business sense; it is often a required part of the materials most academic libraries will have to supply to their institutional review board (IRB), also known in some organization as the ethical review board—the organization responsible for overseeing any testing of human subjects. The IRB will not only want to know the methods you are using to advertise for test subject volunteers, they may also need to approve the specific wording of all advertisements. Comprehensive general information is available from the U.S. Department of Health and Human Services Web site (www.hhs.gov/ohrp/). Most university IRBs also have their own Web presence. One thing is certain: Given the power and importance of IRBs throughout the academic setting, each part of the usability process—including recruitment of test participants—should begin with them in mind.

Marketing Like a Business

Advertising for recruitment is an integral part of your usability testing, not an afterthought. Just as the usability test itself takes careful planning, so too

77

should your advertising strategy. Your final usability project plan should have a section devoted to marketing for test participant recruitment. This should not be just a single sentence ("Post signs around the library asking for testing volunteers."); it should be a well-thought-out marketing strategy, answering all the questions that would be answered in such a strategy in the business world:

- Who are my users?
- Where can I find them?
- What need or want do they have that the library can fulfill?
- Do I have a budget? If so, how much, and how much am I willing to spend per test subject?
- What materials—for both advertising and incentives—will I need?

Know Your Users

What type of users are you looking for? Too often—particularly if the usability working group has not put together a complete action plan—the answer is any! But it is useful, even vital, to decide beforehand exactly who the primary users of your site are (e.g., graduate students, faculty, undergraduates) and focus on recruiting them. The identity of the primary users group will determine where and how you direct your marketing efforts.

Advertising to Attract Users

Librarians tend to be poor marketers. Our products are useful, but not often exciting. Even when the products *are* exciting ("I didn't know I could do that on the library Web site!"), it is very difficult to get that across in our marketing. Advertising for test participants can be facilitated by following a few basic rules:

1. *Lead with your best material.* Some headlines to avoid might be: "Help improve the library Web site!" or "Library seeking test participants." Neither will catch the eye of the average college student. A better strategy is to focus on what you are doing for them: "MAKE $10 IN AN HOUR! (for helping us improve our Web site)" or "EXTRA CREDIT AVAILABLE! (for giving us your opinion on our site)." Advertise like a business, not like a library.
2. *Use attractive keywords and descriptions.* "Testing" is a turnoff for the average student. See rule #1.
3. *Make it easy to contact you from an advertisement.* If you are hanging paper advertisements, use pull-off tabs at the bottom with your contact information. If you are advertising on the Web, create a form for users to get in touch with you. Few students will bother remembering or writing down your contact information.

4. *Let them know that you are seeking their opinion.* Most people are hard-wired to *want* to share their opinions—they tend to like taking surveys or commenting on blogs and discussion boards. If you can get across to students that you are not testing them, but seeking their opinions, your recruiting efforts will bear much more fruit.

Where Should I Advertise?

Most libraries will answer this question with a single answer: "In the library." There are many places in the library that should not be overlooked (e.g., bulletin boards, restrooms, service desks), but your library is not the extent of your business (particularly your Web business). Try to make a list in your mind of businesses that do not advertise outside of their physical premises, and you will probably come up with a pretty short list. Libraries are part of a community, and advertising should focus not on the library alone, but on the entire community that the library serves. The important thing here is to go where the students are. Student newspapers are an option, but ad space there usually is not free, and results tend to be mixed. Try to advertise in all the places outside the library where students tend to congregate: Student union, dorms, dining hall, local and campus coffee shops, department offices, classrooms and classroom buildings, the graduate students' lounge—the list is endless and will vary greatly depending on your campus community and the user group(s) you hope to attract.

Also keep in mind virtual spaces: Many libraries now have a MySpace or FaceBook presence, and if you do not, creating one is easy. The success (if any) of this method of recruitment may in itself provide useful data, as it would indicate that the library's Web 2.0 efforts do not go unnoticed. Failure of these efforts to produce test participants, however, is not necessarily indicative of a general failure of Web 2.0—it is always possible that students who notice, or even appreciate, these attempts are not interested in participating in usability testing.

Advertising on the library Web site should be a given. Many libraries have a news section of the homepage, and this is of course a good (and free) place to advertise. If you have a mechanism for posting surveys on your homepage, this could be a very effective advertising method: It is generally a lot easier to get students to take an online survey than it is to get them into the library for a usability test, but surveys might be a good way to find students who are interested in helping out more. Try posting a short, simple survey on your homepage, with an option to leave a phone number or e-mail address for those willing to help out further ("You can help us further redesign our Web site, and get some free stuff! Let us know if you're interested!!"). Even if none are, you will still have the additional feedback from the survey, and it has cost you nothing.

As in business marketing, sometimes the most effective method of recruitment is the hard sell. This involves going to places where students tend to socialize rather than study, approaching random students, and asking them if they would like to help you redesign the Web site. This approach worked particularly well in the coffee shop when combined with free coffee coupons. "We're giving away three free coffee coupons to students willing to help us redesign the library Web site" worked well, especially when it was pointed out that "that's a 15-dollar value for about a half hour of easy work!"

Working with Others to Attract Subjects

Again, the library does not stand on its own; it is a vital part of the entire campus community. Always be on the lookout for opportunities to partner with groups outside of the usability working group, both inside and outside the library. Libraries with a marketing or external relations department or a marketing committee should make use of that group's expertise and experience to attract subjects. Because these groups already work with students and faculty regularly, they may even have incentives available to offer students. But even if no such entity exists, there are other groups within the library and on campus that can help greatly in recruiting efforts.

The Instruction Department

The instruction department has the advantage of addressing large groups of students at a time within the library, and can be particularly helpful if your test is geared towards undergraduates. See if they would be willing to hand out flyers for you, or to give you a minute or so at the end of their instruction sessions to describe the usability testing and ask for volunteers.

Reference Librarians

Reference librarians work with students more than anyone else in the library, and can help you target specific groups of potential test participants by, for example, mentioning the testing to psychology or computer science students, both of whom might be more interested in such testing than other undergraduates.

Graduate Students

Graduate students tend to rely on the library more than undergraduates, and for that reason may be more willing to help improve the Web research services that the library provides. Graduate students also tend to have established opinions about the library's Web interface, with well-thought-out suggestions on how to better serve researchers (or, at the very least, specific complaints about the layout and navigation of the library's Web site).

At its core, usability testing is an element of human-computer interaction, a blending of psychology with computer science. Graduate students in these areas may be particularly receptive to recruitment efforts, and while their test results (particularly those of computer science majors, who will generally fall outside of the category of "typical user" and into the realm of "power user") should perhaps not be given the same weight as other users, they themselves can be a valuable recruitment tool. (Additionally, these students—particularly those in psychology—may be interested in assisting with giving the usability tests. Because they may have some background in similar testing, and probably no involvement in the design of the Web site, they are perfect candidates for facilitating the usability tests.)

Faculty

It may be possible to convince the faculty in some disciplines to offer extra credit to students who volunteer to participate in usability testing. Even without giving extra credit, faculty who work regularly with the library may be willing to mention the testing in class or hand out a flyer about it. A little faculty involvement can go a long way in these situations. To sell the idea to faculty members, remember to focus on the fact that these tests are designed to make it easier for students to perform research and complete their coursework. Unlike in the business world, where the role of usability testing is to maximize sales, usability testing in academic libraries exists to facilitate student research and to help the library support the teaching faculty. The more this point can be stressed to the faculty, the more they may be willing to assist in test subject recruitment.

81

Current Test Participants

A single test subject can lead to many more. One comment heard consistently from test participants is, "Wow, that was really painless." I always respond to this the same way: "Tell your friends!" Have business cards or flyers ready at the end of a test and ask subjects if they will recruit a friend or two to participate as well. Most are very agreeable to this, especially if there are incentives involved. Also, students who volunteered for your new branch Web site usability test might be willing to help out with your OPAC redesign, too. Keep a list of volunteers' e-mail addresses—you might need to reuse them in a pinch.

It is important to note that this recruitment method could potentially skew your test results by creating a homogenous test subject pool. This should not keep you from using the technique (after all, the more participants the better), but you should be careful to keep their comments in perspective and make every effort to continue recruitment, even if it means testing more subjects than your original plan calls for. Every test subject is valuable, but if 30 percent of your test participants are economics majors, do not be surprised if your results show an overwhelming agreement among your users to put all of your economics databases on the homepage.

Branches and Subject Librarians

Due to their narrower focus, the faculty and staff at branch libraries often work more closely with students or professors than those at "main" libraries (it was much easier to recruit students for the architecture site usability test than for the main library site). These students also might feel a greater vested interest in having an effective, user-friendly Web site, and therefore be more likely to help out. Even if your branch libraries do not have an independent Web presence, their librarians' closer relationships with library users might make subject recruitment easier.

Similarly, subject librarians often have particular students (especially grad students) with whom they work on a regular basis. Ask your subject librarians to pass along requests for help with the usability tests; most will have at least one student they know might be interested.

Student Workers

Obviously, the more average a test participant is, the more valuable their test results will be. On the other hand, the library student worker pool is an easily accessible resource to mine for test participants. Though they may have more than the average understanding of library workings and terminology, they can still provide valuable insights into new interface designs, particularly at the early stages. What is important here is unfamiliarity with the material being tested. A student whose work requires constant use of the library online catalog probably will not be a good subject for testing a new catalog interface. But a student worker from the preservation department, whose sole job is binding books for eight hours a week, might be a fine addition to round out an otherwise skimpy list of participants. The key here is not to stuff the participants list with library workers (or dining hall workers, or bookstore workers). As long as the participants are as representative of your user group as possible, your results also will be representative and your time well spent.

Incentives

If you have a budget, getting incentives is easy; there is an endless list of things students might want enough to give up an hour of their time. However, many of us are not lucky enough to have a usability budget and need to use a little imagination to attract student participants.

Gift Certificates and Coupons

Many retail establishments and restaurants have small budgets set aside for donations. Campus coffee shops might be willing to donate coupons to the library, as might the university bookstore. Moving off-campus, Borders Books and AMC Movie Theaters are generally happy to provide coupons or gift certificates, and there are probably many other businesses in your area that would love the free advertising. Do not think you are asking for a handout by hitting these businesses up for donations—there is plenty in it for them. When a business donates a gift certificate for you to give to a student, not only does their generosity result in guaranteed extra foot traffic, but smart businesses know that they will almost certainly make more money back than they donate. That is why so many are happy to give away gift certificates rather than merchandise.

Look around the Library

Does your library charge for printing and photocopies? If so, a coupon or copy card for free copies or printouts might be feasible. Perhaps you can offer to forgive overdue fines. On one occasion, my library's marketing committee put on an event and had some leftover gift bags of pencils, pens, erasers, and other miscellaneous school supplies, and we were able to use even these simple items to help bring in participants. You do not have to offer them much, just something for their time.

The Greatest Gift of All: Extra Credit

If you can get teaching faculty on board, extra credit is a practically foolproof way to get students interested. This method might be particularly successful if you are designing a Web site with a particular user group in mind (like a government information site for political science majors or a branch Web site).

I Have a Budget—What Now?

If you have a recruitment budget, you will need to decide how you can spend it to maximize results. Unfortunately, there is no one-size-fits-all approach to this. In an informal poll of graduate students and resident assistants at my university, several students said that cash ($10–15 for an hour-long test) was the preferred incentive. Others suggested that something more specific, like bookstore or coffee shop gift certificates, might catch a potential subject's eye better.

Drawings for bigger ticket items (an iPod Nano, for example), with participation in usability testing as the price of entry, also might help attract participants. One usability practitioner had poor results with this method but, coupled with other incentives, it could stimulate more student interest ("Win a free iPod" certainly appears to be a winning phrase for the spam and online advertising markets, and could work in libraries as well).

Location and Scheduling

If possible, perform your usability testing in a location close to where your subjects are. For some, this will be the library. For others—particularly for those testing only a portion of their site or a branch library Web site—it may be somewhere else on campus. My library had much more success recruiting students for usability testing on our architecture studies Web site when we changed the location of the test from the main library to the architecture library. Although the two libraries are only a 10- or 15-minute walk apart, students did not want to go out of their way to participate. Even libraries that have a usability lab may have more success conducting other types of testing (e.g., card sorting or focus group interviews) outside of the library.

Flexibility in scheduling the usability testing also may help recruit and retain potential subjects. The easiest time for library staff to perform testing tends to be during the day, but that may not be the optimum time for students to participate. Avoid putting a testing time (or even a contact time) on your advertisements and let the subjects suggest their own times. This can also help with reliability.

Conclusion

Recruiting test participants is a vital part of usability testing, yet too often it is handled as an afterthought. Remember that without test participants, there can be no tests. Recruitment should be a major part of your testing plan and is a required element in the initial report to the IRB, a step necessary on most campuses to engage in human subject testing of any sort. Additionally, though recruitment of any of your potential user groups in an academic setting—undergraduates, grad students, and faculty—is never easy, you can increase you success rate dramatically by following some basic principles of marketing and using a little creativity.

Chapter 10

Low-Cost Usability Recording

Martin Courtois

Introduction

Many libraries conduct usability tests to evaluate their Web site and obtain feedback from users. Before beginning usability testing, one needs to have a method for recording users' responses. In cases such as card sorting or open-ended testing, it may be sufficient to ask users to fill out a questionnaire or have someone write down users' responses. For task-oriented testing, where a user is asked to use a Web-connected computer to perform a task or locate specific information on the site, it is difficult for an observer to accurately record a user's cursor movements, pages visited, and comments. Video cameras are often used to record tests, but may not produce a clear image of the screen and cursor movements. In addition, video recording requires equipment (camera, tripod) and an operator, which may impede the testing process.

Since the tests will be conducted at a computer, why not use the computer to record the test and create a "video" file that can be played back and analyzed? TechSmith's Morae (www.techsmith.com) is the premier usability recording software, and does a great job of capturing screen activity, as well as audio and video of the test participant. Morae also has tools to facilitate analyzing users' responses. But this capability comes at a price: about $1,200 for a single user license. An alternative product, Hyperionics' HyperCam, gives excellent results when used to record usability tests and can be purchased for less than $40. Similar software is available, such as TechSmith's Camtasia ($299) and a recorder-only version of Morae ($195), but HyperCam provides reliable operation at the lowest cost.

This chapter gives details on configuring HyperCam software, selecting and testing a microphone, using HyperCam during usability tests, and playing back and analyzing recordings. Instructions and settings are for Windows XP, but are similar for Windows 2000.

About HyperCam

HyperCam captures action from a Windows screen—cursor movements, mouse clicks, pages visited—and saves it to an AVI (Audio-Video Interleaved) movie file. Sound from a microphone is also recorded and synchronized with screen actions. This makes it possible to record all screen selections made by test participants, along with a moderator's questions and participants' responses, and play them back.

HyperCam is shareware produced by Hyperionics Technology and is available only for the Windows operating system. Specific system requirements are not provided, but the software has performed without a problem when tested on typically configured XP and Windows 2000 laptops. Information on downloading and installing HyperCam is available on the Hyperionics Web site (www.hyperionics.com), where the software can be registered for $39.95. HyperCam (current version, 2.13) is about a 900 Kb download and 1.2 MB fully installed. An FAQ and message board, e-mail, and phone support are provided.

Configuring HyperCam

Before using HyperCam, it is necessary to configure the software for optimal results. Once installed, launch HyperCam by selecting Start/Programs/HyperCam. The HyperCam window, which contains many of the configuration settings, opens. The following sections refer to settings grouped under the HyperCam window's tabs: Screen Area, Hot Keys, AVI File, Sound, and Other Options. All settings are saved automatically.

86

Screen Area

The recording should be configured to include the scroll bar, browser buttons, and other navigation tools. This is done by specifying the part of the screen to be recorded. Before setting the screen capture area in HyperCam, make sure the display on the computer is set to the resolution to be used during testing. This can be adjusted by pressing Start, then selecting Settings/Control Panel/Display/Settings. Under "Screen Resolution," move the slider to the desired resolution.

Once the desired resolution has been set, open the browser to be used during testing, then open HyperCam. In the HyperCam window, click the Screen Area tab, then the Select Region button. The HyperCam window disappears, and one sees the browser window and crosshairs controlled by the mouse. Move the crosshairs to the upper left corner of the region to be recorded, click, and release. Then move the crosshairs to the lower right corner and click again. The HyperCam window will reappear.

To ensure that recording is unobtrusive, uncheck the boxes to show a blinking rectangle around the recorded area. Check the "Iconize HyperCam Window to the Task Bar" box (see Figure 10.1).

Figure 10.1: Screen Area

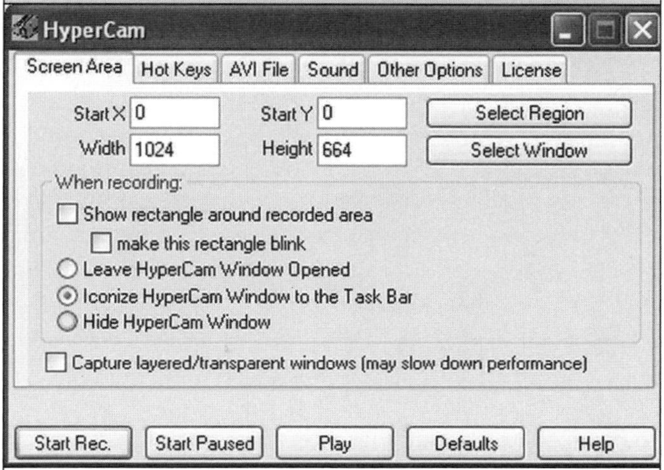

Reproduced with permission of Hyperionics Technology, LLC. You may download a trial version of HyperCam from Hyperionics Web site: www.hyperionics.com

Hot Keys

It is useful to have a single "hot key" to start and stop recording. The default setting is F2; it probably won't be necessary to change this (see Figure 10.2). If the entire browser window is being recorded, the pan function won't be needed.

AVI File

This is the key configuration screen, so check settings carefully.

AVI File Name. Select the path and a generic filename. It is advisable to have a directory set up for each test session and to use the "Browse" button to select the appropriate folder. Files will be large, as much as 10 Mb per minute of recording. It is easy to record the sessions on a networked drive, but if this is not possible, record the sessions on the computer's local drive, then copy files to CD, DVD, or USB drive for later viewing.

Add Sequential Number to the File Name. Check this box. With this feature, HyperCam automatically appends a sequential number to the generic file name (clip0001.avi, clip0002.avi, etc.) and saves the file each time HyperCam recording is stopped. This automatic process is quicker and easier than trying to type in new file names during test sessions.

Record Sound. Check this box. Additional configurations for sound are made under the "Sound" tab.

Figure 10.2: Hot Keys

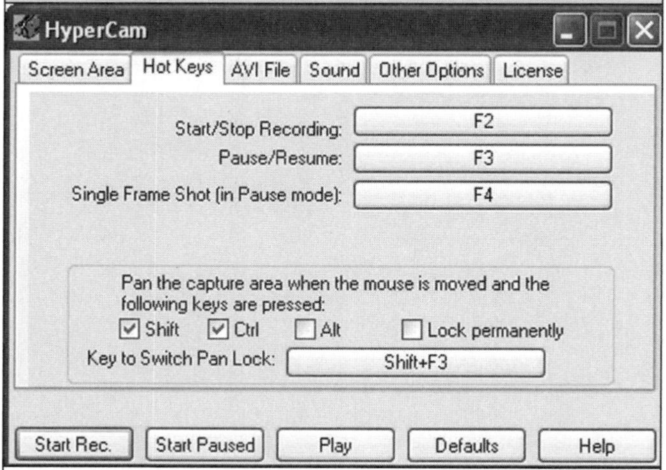

Reproduced with permission of Hyperionics Technology, LLC. You may download a trial version of HyperCam from Hyperionics Web site: www.hyperionics.com.

Rate in Frames per Second. Both record and playback should be set to 10.

Cursor/Full Frame Capture Ratio. Change to 3. This means that only every third frame will be captured from the screen. For other frames, only cursor position is updated. Since participants will be working on static Web pages, it is unlikely any data will be lost. Even with this setting, full frames are captured about every .33 seconds, often enough for even the fastest mouse clicker!

Key Frame. Keep at 100 frames. This means every hundredth frame is captured in its entirety. For intervening frames, only the differences between the current and preceding frames are captured. Changing this value may make it difficult to edit the AVI files.

Frame Compression Quality. Keep at 75 percent (see Figure 10.3). This will produce crystal-clear recordings, although files will be large. To reduce file size, change this setting to 50 percent; recordings will still be legible, though not as clear.

Sound

Make sure the "Record Sound" box is checked. Set "Sample Size" to 16 bit and "Sample Rate" to 11025 (see Figure 10.4). This gives acceptable performance for recording participants' comments without inflating file sizes. One

Figure 10.3: AVI File

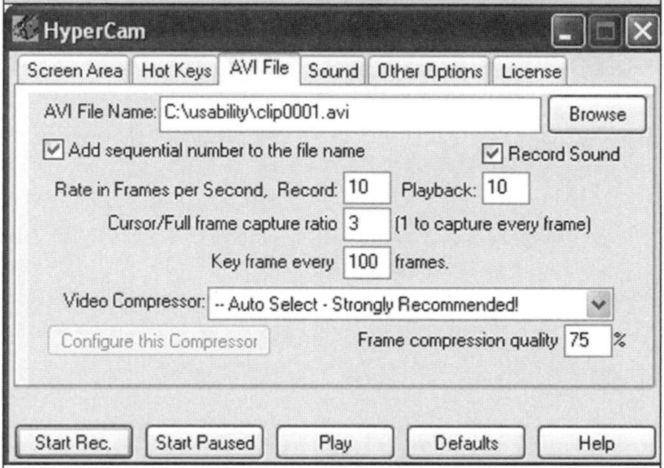

Reproduced with permission of Hyperionics Technology, LLC. You may download a trial version of HyperCam from Hyperionics Web site: www.hyperionics.com

Figure 10.4: Sound

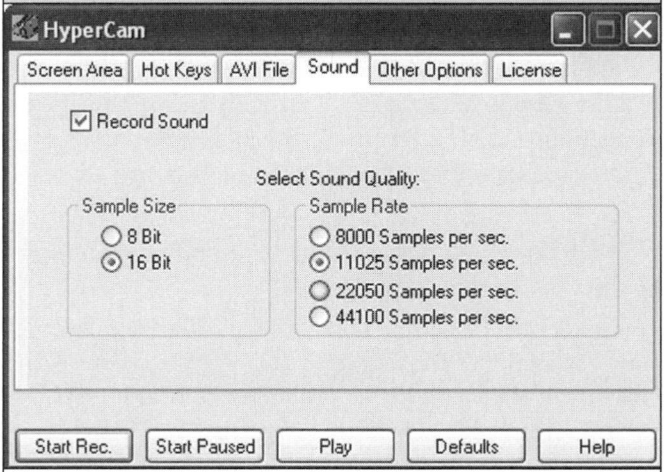

Reproduced with permission of Hyperionics Technology, LLC. You may download a trial version of HyperCam from Hyperionics Web site: www.hyperionics.com

does not need CD quality, but it is important to be able to decipher what users are saying.

Figure 10.5: Other Options

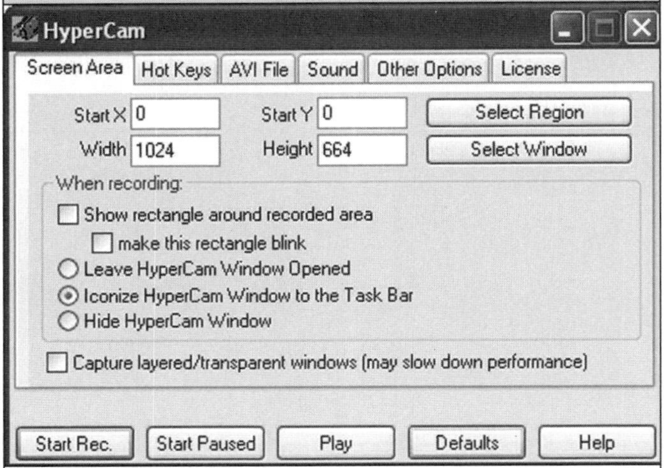

Reproduced with permission of Hyperionics Technology, LLC. You may download a trial version of HyperCam from Hyperionics Web site: www.hyperionics.com

Other Options

Make sure the "Record Cursor" box is checked (see Figure 10.5). The "starburst" feature makes it easy to determine when a participant clicks the left or right mouse button. The starburst is visible only on playback and helps determine if the participant actually clicked on a link or only hovered over it. To include an audible click in recordings when the user makes a mouse click, move the "Mouse click sound volume" slider to the right.

Other Settings

Color Mode

Modern computers can display millions of colors. This is a real boon for most applications, but increases file sizes and can slow the recording process. To keep file sizes manageable, set the color mode as low as possible. To do this, click Start, then select Settings/Control Panel/Display. Click on the "Settings" tab, and under "Color Quality," select the lowest setting, for instance, "Medium 16 bit." Be sure to restore this setting after the test session.

Hardware Acceleration

On older computers, HyperCam may drop some frames, segments of the audio may be lost, and audio and video may not remain in sync. If more than 50 percent of frames are dropped, an error message will display. To correct this problem, click Start and select Settings/Control Panel/Display. Click the "Settings" tab, then the "Advanced" button. Click the "Troubleshooting" tab. Under "Hardware Acceleration," move the slider all the way to the left, toward "None." This will help keep the graphics display in sync with the slower processor. Be sure to restore this setting after the test session.

About Microphones

Having a record of participants' comments is a useful tool in analyzing usability tests, but some configuring is needed to obtain an audible recording. Follow these guidelines to get the best recording.

Use a Cheap Microphone

Sound cards on Windows computers are designed to work with three-conductor, 3.5 mm (⅛") plugs typically found on inexpensive desktop computer microphones (see Figure 10.6). This wiring scheme is typically used to supply low-voltage DC power to the microphone, resulting in a strong signal to the sound card. These plugs have two black stripes around the circumference of the shaft; plugs with only one stripe will not work as well. Professional-quality microphones use a different wiring scheme and usually do not produce a strong enough signal without an external preamplifier (Guerra, 2006). For ease of use and a good recording, the Logitech Desktop Microphone (980240-0403) is an excellent choice. It is available from many online retailers for about $10.

USB-powered microphones, such as the LogiTech USB Desktop Microphone (980186-0403), are popular and available for about $20. In the author's testing, the LogiTech USB microphone produced an acceptable signal but not as strong as the conventional microphone. USB microphones require a slightly different setup, as described in the USB Microphone section.

91

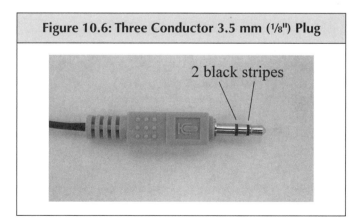

Figure 10.6: Three Conductor 3.5 mm (⅛") Plug

2 black stripes

Adjust the Recording Volume

Conventional Microphone (3.5mm plug)

Plug the microphone into the microphone input on the computer. This input may be marked with an image of a microphone and is usually red or pink in color.

To get a good sound recording, turn on the "Mic Boost." This gives extra amplification to the microphone signal. It also will be necessary to adjust the record level to ensure a good recording and the playback level to hear the recording. This can be a tricky process; the steps outlined below should be followed carefully.

In Windows, click Start, then select Settings/Control Panel/Sound and Audio Devices. In the "Sound and Audio Devices Properties" dialog box, make sure the "Volume" tab is selected. In the "Device volume" section, perform these steps:

1. Set the "Device volume" slider to about ¾.
2. Make sure the "Mute" box is unchecked.
3. Check the "Place volume icon in the taskbar" if the ability to adjust the playback volume from the Taskbar is desired.
4. Click the "Advanced" button.

A "Volume Control" dialog box should open. If there is a channel for Microphone with an "Advanced" button at the bottom of the channel (Figure 10.7), the next four steps can be skipped. If there is not a Microphone

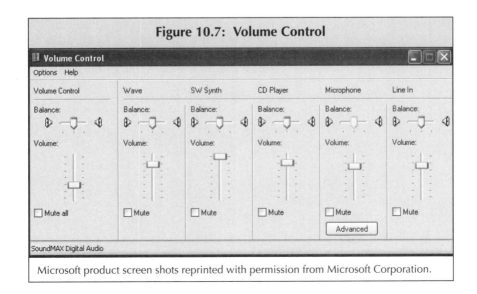

Figure 10.7: Volume Control

Microsoft product screen shots reprinted with permission from Microsoft Corporation.

channel, or the Microphone channel lacks the "Advanced" button, follow these steps:

1. In the "Volume Control" dialog box (see Figure 10.7), select Options/ Properties.
2. A "Properties" dialog box will open (see Figure 10.8). Click the radio button next to "Playback." Make sure the box next to "Microphone" or "Mic" is checked.
3. Click the radio button next to "Recording." Make sure the box next to "Microphone" or "Mic" is checked.
4. Click the radio button for "Playback" again. Click OK.

An "Advanced" button should now be visible at the bottom of the Microphone channel in the "Volume Control" dialog box (see Figure 10.7). Make sure the "Mute" button is not checked. Set the slider in the Microphone channel to about ¾. Click the "Advanced" button. In the "Advanced Controls for Microphone" dialog box (see Figure 10.9), make sure the box next to "MIC Boost" is checked. This may be labeled as "Microphone Boost" or "+20db Gain." Click Close.

Figure 10.8: Properties Dialog Box

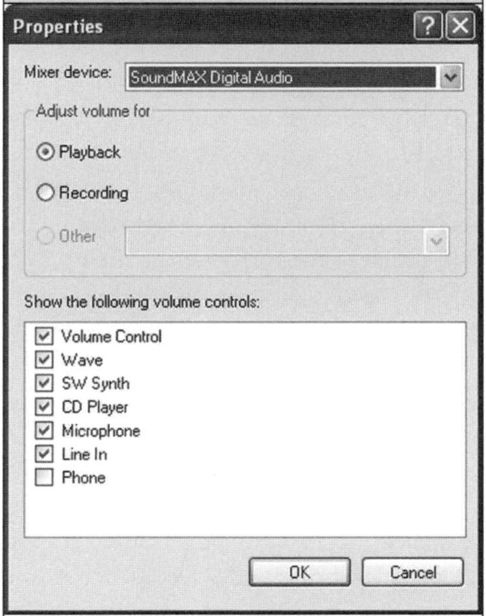

Microsoft product screen shots reprinted with permission from Microsoft Corporation.

Figure 10.9: Advanced Controls for Microphone

Advanced Controls for Microphone ☒

These settings can be used to make fine adjustments to your audio.

Tone Controls

These settings control how the tone of your audio sounds.

Bass: Low ———————— High

Treble: Low ———————— High

Other Controls

These settings make other changes to how your audio sounds. See your hardware documentation for details.

☑ 1 MIC Boost

[Close]

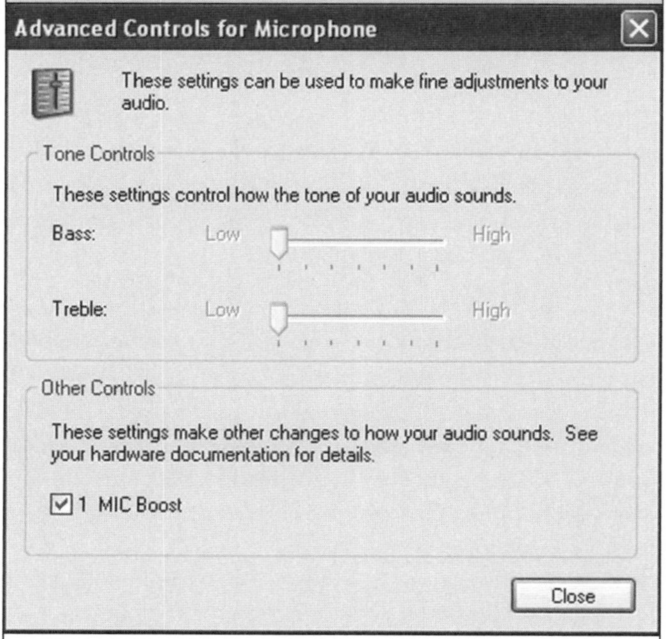

Microsoft product screen shots reprinted with permission from Microsoft Corporation.

The "Volume Control" dialog box should now be displayed (see Figure 10.7). Select Options/Properties. Click the radio button next to "Recording." Click OK. The "Recording Control" dialog box should be visible (see Figure 10.10). In the Microphone channel, make sure the box next to "Select" is checked, and set the slider about ¾. Close the dialog box. On the "Sounds and Audio Devices Properties" dialog box, click OK. Close the Control Panel.

The microphone should now be ready to test.

USB Microphone

Plug the microphone into a USB port on the computer. Turn on the mic if required (the LogiTech mic has an on/off switch on the base).

In Windows, click Start, then select Settings/Control Panel/Sound and Audio Devices, then click the "Audio" tab. Under "Sound Recording," pull down the "Default Device" window and select the microphone. With the LogiTech mic, the selection is "AK5370," the analog-to-digital converter chipset used in the mic. Check the documentation supplied with other mic models for the correct selection. Click "Apply." Under "Sound Recording," click the

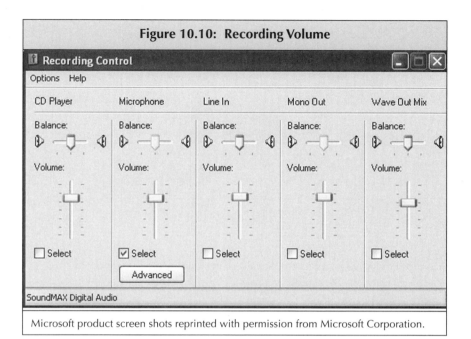

Figure 10.10: Recording Volume

Microsoft product screen shots reprinted with permission from Microsoft Corporation.

"Volume" button. This will open a volume control for "Wave In." Adjust the volume slider all the way up and make sure the "Mute All" box is unchecked. Close the "Wave In" dialog box and click OK.

Test the Microphone (Conventional and USB Mics)

Click Start, then select Programs/Accessories/Entertainment/Sound Recorder. Click the red button to begin recording, and speak into the microphone. The green line should react to the sounds. If the green line thickens only a little bit, raise the microphone volume slider in the Recording Control window (see Figure 10.10), or move the microphone closer. If the green line grows to fill the entire window, lower the volume. Figure 10.11 shows a strong microphone signal. Use the Sound Recorder controls to stop, rewind, and play the recording. Use the Volume Control window to adjust the playback volume. Using Sound Recorder to test the microphone and set the recording level helps ensure that HyperCam will produce legible recordings.

The Sound Recorder recording was probably made at the default, 8-bit sample size, resulting in some static during playback. In HyperCam, the sample size was changed to 16 bit; playback will be much clearer.

To avoid feedback (a high pitched, squealing sound coming from the computer's speakers) while recording with HyperCam, turn off the speakers or use the Volume Control (see Figure 10.7) to turn down the playback volume. If

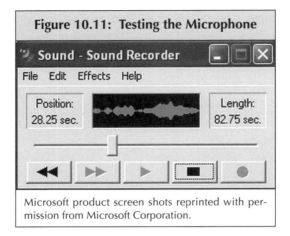

Figure 10.11: Testing the Microphone

Microsoft product screen shots reprinted with permission from Microsoft Corporation.

the moderator and subject are seated at the computer during the testing, the top of the monitor is usually a good location for the microphone. If using a laptop, position the microphone so participants are speaking into it as they look at the screen.

Using HyperCam

With both sound and video elements, there is much to configure in Hypercam. Be sure to test the system thoroughly prior to conducting actual usability testing sessions.

During the test, it is likely that several questions will be posed to each participant. Since the .avi files generated by HyperCam will be large, create a file for each question. This will facilitate handling files if it is necessary to copy them to a CD, or comparing responses to the same question from different participants. Plan ahead by creating a directory structure and file naming scheme, particularly if more than one moderator is conducting tests.

To begin recording:

- open the browser window
- open HyperCam
- minimize HyperCam

The HyperCam icon will be visible at the bottom of the screen. To begin recording, press F2 (or other Start/Stop "hot key" configured in the HyperCam setup). The camera lens in the HyperCam icon will change from blue to red to signal that HyperCam is recording. Press F2 again to stop recording, and the camera lens changes back to blue.

By using F2 to start and stop recording, it is easy for the moderator to control the creation of a new .avi file for each question. Simply press F2 to begin recording and press it again to stop recording. HyperCam automatically appends a sequential number to the file name and saves the file, so it will not be necessary to interrupt the test to save files and enter file names.

In addition to starting and stopping the recording, the test moderator will need to elicit comments from the participant to get the person to think out loud. This sounds easy but in fact can be one of the most challenging aspects of conducting tests and getting usable data. The moderator should have prepared questions to pose to the participant as the situation demands, such as these examples:

- Why did you click on that link?
- What did you expect to find on this page?
- What would have made that information easier to find?
- You look puzzled . . . tell me what you're thinking.

Try to put the subject at ease. Emphasize that the Web site is being tested, not the participant's skill in finding information. Chat with the subject for a few minutes before the test begins, or perhaps offer some refreshment, to make them feel comfortable. However, participants may "freeze up" during the test, so be ready with questions to help generate comments and suggestions. Despite the moderator's best efforts, some participants simply may not have many comments. Do not add to their stress by repeating questions if they are not responding. It is likely a quiet subject will be balanced by one who has much to say. Role-playing a test session can give moderators a chance to practice interacting with participants and prompting for comments.

Playback

There are a number of ways to play back recordings, but to produce a clear image it is important that video be rendered at 100 percent. The latest versions of programs such as Windows Media Player and RealPlayer have an option to display video at 100 percent, but even with this setting, the image is usually blurry.

One solution is to run Media Player in version 6.4 mode, which will play .avi files at 100 percent. Use Windows Explorer to locate the file mplayer2.exe in the Program Files/Windows Media Player folder. Double click the filename and Media Player 6.4 will open. Select File/Open, then click the Browse button and locate an .avi file to play. Double click the filename, then click OK. Under View, use the Full Screen and Zoom options to adjust the size of the playback.

The best solution, however, is to download and install the free Camtasia Player from TechSmith (www.techsmith.com/camtasia/accessories/player.asp). Camtasia Player always plays back videos at 100 percent and gives the clearest image of any of the players.

97

Be sure the resolution on the playback computer is set to the same size as or larger than the recording computer. For example, if the computer used to record is set for 1024×768 resolution, the playback computer should be set for the same resolution or higher (e.g., 1280×1024).

Analyzing Results

Analyzing results and deciding how to revise the Web site are major tasks and beyond the scope of this chapter. However, a few points regarding viewing usability test recordings may be in order:

- *Watch the playback.* After a testing session, most moderators come away with distinct impressions of where users were having problems. It is great to have that insight, but do not rely only on those first impressions. Viewing recordings of the tests more than once will help identify problem areas.
- *Juggle playback order.* In addition to viewing recordings in order by test participant, try viewing all recordings in order by test question. This will make it easier to focus on specific aspects of the Web site addressed in the test questions.
- *Do both quantitative and qualitative analyses.* How many users were able to answer a question successfully? How long did it take for them to complete a task? How many clicks? Users' comments allow for more of a qualitative analysis: Where were users having problems? Where did users seem confused or uncertain? These impressions may reveal problems not apparent in a quantitative analysis.
- *Work in a group.* Library Web teams may want to watch and discuss the playback together. Try to define problems users are having, then brainstorm for solutions. Even better, set up focus groups and involve your users in identifying solutions.
- Get department heads and administrators to watch the videos. Anyone involved in testing knows how eye-opening it is to observe someone using your site in a completely unexpected manner. Share that experience with those who can provide resources for development and testing.

Conclusion

HyperCam is an inexpensive way to record users' screen movements and verbal comments during task-oriented usability testing. The software is easy to use and enables a single person to conduct the test session and control the recording. Some attention to detail is required in configuring HyperCam, particularly in terms of microphone selection and recording levels, and advance planning is needed to be able to handle the large files produced recording.

With this preparation done, HyperCam is unobtrusive during testing and provides a more thorough and detailed record of the session than handwritten notes or video recording. A HyperCam recording of the session is of immense value in reviewing and analyzing test results, particularly in terms of conveying the full impact of the session to colleagues who did not observe the test first-hand. With HyperCam, it is possible for a library to develop a usability testing program using existing hardware and with almost no software costs.

Reference

Guerra, Luis. 2006. "Interfacing Professional Microphones to Computer Sound Cards." Available: www.shure.com/ProAudio/Products/us_pro_ea_connectingmics

Chapter 11

Communicating Usability Results Effectively

Brenda Reeb

Introduction

Usability test results need to be shared with interface designers or programmers if the results are going to be incorporated in subsequent design iterations. This chapter discusses popular formats that the usability practitioner can use to share test findings and what elements to include in each format. A second type of communication is less obvious but equally important. In libraries where usability techniques are new to most staff, reporting results may not be enough. Staff may need background information on how the tests work before they will trust test results. Practitioners who take time to explain usability practices to their colleagues have more success incorporating findings into design. Staff won't support something that they do not understand. Novice usability practitioners commonly underestimate the amount of communication needed to gain staff buy-in for usability.

Types of Results and Findings

Before discussing communication formats, it is helpful to define a few examples of the types of usability findings that surface during a test session. Design problems and user behavior patterns discovered in a round of usability testing are sometimes called "findings" instead of "results." The word "results" implies an absolute correctness, which is usually inaccurate in describing the data that surface during a test session. Any staff members who are responsible for interpreting usability findings must carefully distinguish among *observation*, *opinion*, and *design* recommendation.

Here is an example of an observation recorded in response to a test question asking the user to "Find an article on film noir for your English writing class."

- *She typed the keywords "film noir" into the library catalog search box.*

Now, librarians know that articles are not found in the catalog. Several possible opinions of this user's action might be:

- *She knows what the catalog is and believes articles are found there.*
- *She does not know what the catalog is and believes she is searching every single resource the library owns, including articles.*
- *She knows how databases and articles work but does not see the Find Articles search box in the lower right corner of the page.*

Which opinion is correct? If the user did not think aloud during her action, and the test moderator chose not to ask what her motivations were, we do not know the user's reasons for typing keywords to find articles in the library catalog. Facial expressions or mouse activity might provide nonverbal clues. If test observers miss some verbal or nonverbal clues, they might form different opinions on the user's action. If most of the observers share the same opinion, that is a good bet that the opinion is valid. If there is disagreement, it is best to record all of the opinions. Consensus is not the point and need not be pursued.

Design recommendations for this scenario could be:

- *Move the Find Articles search box to the left side of the page so that users realize there is a choice in search boxes.*
- *Make the Find Articles header really big and change the color to give the header prominence.*
- *Add a Find Databases section to the Web site.*

As with opinions, there is no single right answer as to which design recommendation is best. The designer or programmer chooses as best as he or she can and learns in the next round of testing if the design has improved. Carefully distinguish among observation, opinion, and design recommendations when sharing test findings.

Choosing a Report Format

Three popular report formats are verbal, written, and digital media. Each choice has trade-offs in terms of time investment and formality. The best choice is the format that meets the needs of a specific library in terms of time constraints, access to shared file space, and culture of the library.

Verbal

The quickest method of communicating findings, and the least formal, is verbal. For this method to succeed, the designers and programmers need to attend the test sessions as either observers or usability practitioners. Schedule a brief (perhaps 30 minutes) meeting at the conclusion of the last test in the test session so that the testing team can immediately summarize the key findings for that round. During this meeting, everyone who observed the test session shares their observations. The goal of this conversation is to note the major patterns that emerge from everyone's observations and to note the minor observations that occurred but do not form clear patterns. Do not force consensus. No written report or video is produced, except the notes individuals scribble to themselves.

Speed is the most positive attribute of this method. Designers and programmers immediately return to their desks to build the next prototype. Choose the verbal format if you want to test again in a matter of days, not weeks. On the negative side, there is no tangible report to share with staff who did not attend the test sessions. Over time, the findings are subject to memory lapses of the participants. Even with these flaws, this is a great method for experienced staff engaged in very rapid prototyping, perhaps producing a new design iteration each week. Interestingly, it is also a great method for novice practitioners who need practice drawing significant conclusions and seeing patterns in the vast amount of data generated in a test session. Participants learn personal strengths and weaknesses in test interpretation without getting overwhelmed in excessive written reports or having to learn video editing software.

Written

103

Written reports are popular in libraries. Bulleted lists, charts that record the click path of each user for each test question, and narrative summaries are examples of written report formats suitable for usability tests. Try using color-coded text to distinguish observation, opinion, and design recommendations. Written reports provide a permanent reference point when several weeks elapse between design iterations, or when anyone questions the purpose of design elements that appear in subsequent design iterations.

On the negative side, written reports are time intensive to write and read. When deciding between verbal or written formats, or between simple or complex written formats, choose the format that captures the minimum level of detail staff seem to require. It will vary by project and by institution. If staff members habitually complain they lack time for testing, consider briefer reports. If staff members habitually complain that they are not informed of the design work, consider more inclusive written reports and save them to a shared file area so that staff members can read them at their leisure. Generally discourage long, formal reports. This report style runs counter to the spirit of usability testing, which is rapid and iterative. Focus on the test experience and the findings, not on a perfectly presented report.

Digital Media

Digital media formats provide compelling video clips of users. Event-recording software is an easy and inexpensive method to create videos of test sessions. Morae, produced by TechSmith (www.techsmith.com), is one popular example of this software. Event-recording software records a headshot of the user (if you mount the camera on top of the monitor), audio, and desktop activity during the test. This software is easy to edit, so that you can create one continuous clip of a test session or string several brief segments together in a storyboard. Remote viewing is a unique feature of event-recording software. During remote viewing, people can observe tests in a separate room. In this environment, observers can comfortably come and go from the room, eat or drink, and talk amongst themselves without interrupting the test.

Like written reports, video files are time consuming to create and view. However, a key video clip can convey user behavior better than a thousand written words and is worth the investment once library staff decide to use usability in their design process. An issue to consider is the large file size of the videos. Plan a shared file storage system to reduce the need to burn CDs for staff who did not attend the test session.

Using a traditional video camera mounted on a tripod is not worth the effort. This technology does not capture desktop activity or the user's facial expressions. Compared to event-recording software, editing regular video is time consuming.

104

Recording a Description of Each Test Session

In libraries that consistently practice usability, keeping a record of what tests were done when, by whom, and for what project is helpful for future planning and for sharing findings with other libraries. Even if the test session findings were presented verbally, it takes just a few minutes to record basic descriptive data for the test session. For written or video reports, it is easy to include the descriptive data with the report itself. Include the purpose of the test and the design goals. Record the number of test subjects and their status as undergraduate, faculty, or staff. A copy of the test questions and the script should accompany the raw data and the summarized "findings" or results. Save the design prototype for each iteration. Design recommendations based on the analysis and findings and an evaluation of the difficulty of implementing the recommendation vs. the benefit for users are good elements to add to written reports.

Educating Staff about Usability Techniques

While it is obvious that usability findings need to be shared, it is much less obvious that usability practitioners need to explain usability theory and methods to staff unfamiliar with usability. Usability techniques are new in libraries and require explanation. It can take up to a year for a majority of library staff to trust the methods. Staff members unaccustomed to the methodology often misunderstand the work, which can slow down the process and cause unnecessary stress. Until trust is established, plan to explain repeatedly why various methods are proven and reliable.

Findings are qualitative and open to interpretation. Staff and stakeholders who understand the underlying methodology are less apt to challenge usability findings. Three common challenges to usability work are:

1. 3–5 users are not enough.
2. Paper prototypes are amateurish and childish.
3. The detail in a task or test question is faulty, rendering all the findings invalid.

Each of these challenges can be met effectively with a well-designed communication strategy. These criticisms are common in any organization that introduces usability, not just libraries.

A multilayered communication plan works best. Provide an overview perspective on usability for all staff members and address specific issues with smaller audiences. In an overview information session, describe the types of tests planned. Define specialized vocabulary like *heuristic*, *paper prototypes*, and *iteration*. Provide examples as often as possible. Many usability methods are best explained by an example or illustration rather than a lecture. Stage a mock test at a staff meeting, or show two consecutive design iterations and discuss the test findings that influenced the second iteration.

The role of the test moderator may create unique problems in libraries because the role looks similar to the work of reference librarians. Both roles interact with patrons using a structured conversation, and both talk with users about finding content or accomplishing tasks on the library Web site. The roles differ in that the test moderator maintains neutrality and neither teaches nor answers reference questions during a test. Jeff Rubin, in his book *Handbook of Usability Testing* (1994), convincingly explains why neutrality in this role is critical. Any attempt to teach the user the "right way" to complete a task during a test invalidates the test. Good test moderators, unlike good reference librarians, let the teachable moments pass.

Instructional Material for Usability

Several popular usability Web sites and books provide instructional material to counter the major common criticisms of usability. This content is particularly useful for smaller audiences, such as administrators. Jakob Nielsen's Alert Box e-newsletter (www.useit.com/alertbox/) offers brief explanations of usability basics. Popular newsletter issues include "Usability 101," "Return on Investment," and "Why You Only Need to Test With 5 Users." Online Computer Library Center (OCLC) provides a concise treatment of heuristics that includes a chart listing 14 heuristics and instructions for assigning severity and extent (www.oclc.org/policies/usability/heuristic/oclc.htm). Steven Krug uses a graphic style to convey many usability tenets in his book *Don't Make Me Think* (2006), which can persuade skeptics that usability works with only 3–5 users. Keep several of these instructional pieces on hand to share at the appropriate moment.

Conclusion

Without effective communication of usability findings, usability testing will not impact the Web site design. A communication plan, including an instructional program for staff, increases the likelihood of successful Web designs. Choose a communication format (verbal, written, or digital media) that suits your organization and fits with the resources allocated for user interface design.

References

Krug, Steven. 2006. *Don't Make Me Think*. 2nd ed. Berkeley, CA: New Riders.
Rubin, Jeffrey. 1994. *Handbook of Usability Testing*. New York: Wiley.

Usability Case Study: Purdue University Libraries

Hal P. Kirkwood, Jr.

Context

The Purdue libraries were early pioneers of Web development, creating a link-rich site prior to the development of Yahoo! Through the late 1990s, the site was redesigned only once, without user input. Anecdotal evidence from both students and library staff illuminated a severe problem with the site. Complaints focused on the numerous layers within the site, which made it difficult to find useful information in a timely manner. Discussion on the need for a major revision and redesign of the Purdue libraries' Web site ensued. There was no specific group in place to take on such an enormous task, so the Web Site Support Team (WSST) was created to rebuild the Purdue libraries' Web site.

The Purdue libraries team structure was developed in late 1999–2000 to facilitate communication across the library system and improve action on the goals and objectives of the libraries' strategic plan. The initial charge to the WSST was to create an easily navigable, professional, and logically organized Web site for the Purdue University Libraries, which consist of 14 departmental libraries with individual Webmasters for almost every library. Team members, with a variety of experience and knowledge in Web design, were drawn from all over the library system. The team began to plan for a complete revision and redesign of the libraries' Web site. A primary consideration from the very beginning was to include users—students and faculty—throughout the redesign process.

The Testing

Preliminary Research

Initially, the team developed a base of knowledge and expertise among its members by reviewing articles on Web site redesign and information architecture.

107

The team reviewed writings by Instone, Nielsen, Morville, Rosenfeld, and other respected experts in the field. The team also reviewed, compared, and evaluated similar Web sites, looking at other comparable university library systems. Based on the readings and research, a plan was created to guide the redesign.

A sub-team of the WSST was charged with creating and implementing a heuristic test of the current Web site to determine its conformance to commonly accepted Web design standards. The results of the heuristic test showed the site was not adhering to many common design elements and constructs.

Online Survey

An online survey was developed to determine user expectations of the site and general user preferences and technical knowledge. Questions were developed by the team and then tested using student employees within the libraries. This pretest phase was extremely useful for creating an effective tool, allowing the team to refine the questions to ensure the survey was clear and would provide information that could be used to help redesign the site. The final survey was then rolled out on the home page of the libraries' Web site. Several of the departmental libraries also included a link to the survey from their home pages. The survey gave an initial view of users' concerns with the site, a self-perception of their searching abilities, and a scan of their technological position (browser-type, Internet access, etc.).

The online survey, by way of a request for volunteers, also provided the team with a pool of students for the task-oriented testing in the next phase of the redesign. In addition, several advertisements requesting volunteers were placed in the student newspaper. The incentive was a $10 copy card for 20 to 30 minutes of testing. Results from the advertisements were very poor—most of the volunteers came from the option to volunteer in the online survey.

Task-oriented Testing

The task-oriented phase consisted of a series of tests in which students and faculty were observed completing a variety of tasks. These provided information used to help develop prototypes of the site. Student employees were again used to test card sets and questions to ensure they were worded properly and would elicit useful information. In a card sorting test, the terms and sections of the current site were individually placed on cards. A deck of cards was given to a participant who was asked to sort the cards into three piles: Very important, moderately important, and less important. Once this was completed, the piles were taken away for later analysis. A second matching deck was given to the participants who were asked to sort the cards into piles of similar resources that made sense to them. They were then asked to create a label for each pile. Ultimately, the tests showed what was important to the students, what they considered to be related, and what they would call a specific group of resources. They provided insight into how well the libraries were meeting student and faculty expectations of what information they would find and how they would find it.

A second round of task-oriented testing consisted of a series of questions the participants attempted to answer using the current site. A team member would observe them attempting to answer each question and write notes on how they approached finding the answer. A different group of volunteers was used for this round of testing. The participants were asked to think out loud about their impressions and their considerations while trying to answer the questions. The participants were scheduled in small groups and tested simultaneously in an electronic classroom. The purpose of this test was to determine current navigation problems and to shed light on how students and faculty seek information from the site.

In both rounds of task-oriented testing, a brief focus group discussion was held after each session. Participants in the card sorting and the task-based testing were brought together in a small group in which a general discussion was held about the libraries' site and Web site navigation in general. Interestingly, participants often said they preferred one thing while testing showed they preferred the exact opposite.

Findings

The task-based testing found problems in several areas including terminology, navigation, and site architecture. Participants had difficulty understanding library jargon and inconsistent naming of resources and services. They commented on problems navigating the site, including dead-end and orphaned pages. The site architecture was also clearly a problem. In both the task-based testing and the card sort testing, participants reported desiring better, faster access to resources and services. The site had too many layers, forcing multiple clicks to get to useful information.

The team collated the information that had been gathered and determined that it was necessary to focus on several specific design elements. The overall look of the site needed to be refreshed and made more appealing. The navigation needed to be more consistent across the entire site, including the departmental libraries; this led to the use of Cascading Style Sheets to maintain a consistent look with some flexibility for the departmental Webmasters. The site architecture needed to be improved drastically with the creation of a controlled vocabulary, to be used across the site. It was also necessary to create clearer paths between pages and sections to enable visitors to know where they are, where they can go, and how to get back. The original site was far too deep, with an excessive amount of clicking required to find the needed resources.

Finally, the home page needed to become a more effective tool for finding services and resources quickly.

Communicating with the Webmasters

The WSST met with the libraries' Webmasters to discuss the findings and to plan for developing the new site. This provided an opportunity for the Webmasters to provide input as well as to create buy-in to the redesign process. The WSST presented its findings from the testing and led a discussion of the design ramifications of the findings.

Underlying Infrastructure

The underlying infrastructure that formed the foundation for the redesign of the site was created next. A thesaurus was built to resolve issues of inconsistent terminology and excessive jargon. Site architecture was developed to guide the redesign. Visual elements were discussed and samples were created, leading to the development of prototypes.

Prototypes

The WSST then created two subteams, each assigned to create a prototype of the redesigned homepage. It was decided that there was enough variation in the information collected that two separate prototypes should be made and then compared and tested by users. The two teams were each given certain design elements (left side vs. right side navigation; drop down menus vs. scrolling menus; alternate terminology) to create the homepage and a sample lower-level page. Once the prototypes were built, they were shown to users. Participants in the original card sorting and task-oriented testing were contacted and given access to the prototypes, and minor changes were made based on their feedback. The prototypes were then taken to a new group of task-oriented testers. Over a three-week period, the team set up laptops in a variety of public locations, including several of the departmental libraries on campus and several other high-traffic areas. The team solicited more volunteers to sit down and complete several tasks with each prototype and provide commentary on which features they found most useful or implemented most effectively. The team alternated which prototype was tested first to avoid any preference based on testing order. An additional function of this public testing was to promote the redesign project and to highlight the fact that users were involved throughout the process.

Final Redesign

The final redesign consisted of a merged version of the two prototypes. Elements that showed positive results from the final round of testing, as well as the previous testing and research, were brought together for the final redesign. A publicity campaign was developed, and the final design was presented to the libraries' faculty and staff. The design was then rolled out publicly to the faculty and students of the university.

Conclusion

At the conclusion of the project, the team felt very confident it had designed a more user-friendly and user-centered site. The site received very positive feedback once it was rolled out. The team worked with Purdue University marketing so that the color scheme and some design elements were in line with the eventual redesign of the university site. Since the libraries actually implemented their redesign first, it looked like the university was catching up with the library; this was great for the libraries' marketing and campus standing.

Throughout the redesign process, the team focused on involving the libraries' users. The team was aware of numerous complaints and decided to gather input from users to justify the changes. In the past, changes had been made without user input; this had been questioned by the libraries' administration. Keeping the redesign user-centered, with users involved throughout the process, allowed the team to justify every decision it made, so that if challenged it could go back to the tests and the data to support the direction it had chosen.

Web sites are living, adapting entities, and there is a discussion of conducting a new round of usability testing of the Purdue libraries' site to determine if there are any design problems to be corrected. The Web Site Support Team is in a discussion with the new libraries' administration about future development of the Web site. Issues being debated include migration to a content management system or outsourcing the next redesign. Regardless of what is ultimately done, the libraries will always keep their users involved in the design process.

Usability Case Study: University of Virginia

Leslie Johnston

Context

In 2001, the University of Virginia Library was evaluating the methods it used for internal assessment and process evaluation following the adoption of the Balanced Scorecard for library assessment metrics (Self, 2003).[1] The library's Web sites are a key entry point for users to many of the library's collections and services. Ease of use and consistency in design and functionality are key ingredients to building a customer-oriented system. With this in mind, a usability group with representation from various University Library units, the Law Library, and the Health Sciences Library was created to undertake assessment of the library's growing Web presence. This group set up the initial criteria for selecting sites to be tested, procedures and forms to be used in testing, and targets for testing that would represent success.

The usability group is not a department but a standing committee of staff members who are interested in improving the usefulness of online resources. Membership in the usability group is not fixed in terms of numbers, units represented, or term of service. The only constants are that the Management Information Systems and Communications departments of the University Library must be represented, and at least one member must come from both the Law and Health Sciences libraries. The University Library and its branches—the Law Library and the Health Sciences Library—are different administrative units at the University of Virginia, but work in a collaborative way and share a single OPAC and many licensed resources. Members represent many units and roles in the libraries, including cataloging, public services, and systems. The group averages approximately eight members,

113

---

1. For more information on the Balanced Scorecard assessment methodology, see www.balanced scorecard.org/

some who have served since the formation of the group and others who served only three months.

Process

The criteria for sites to be tested were simple. All new sites and any sites scheduled for design revision would be tested. Certain categories of sites—primarily temporary pages and Web-based incarnations of Library exhibits—would not be tested. The University of Virginia Library's Web sites are designed centrally by the communications Web staff, but implementation and maintenance are distributed throughout the Library. Each unit or group within the library that has a Web site is responsible for its content and maintenance.

It was agreed that, depending upon the site to be tested, either heuristic testing or full usability testing might be used. For most sites, full usability testing would be performed. For large and complex sites that include interactive services, both heuristic testing and full usability testing would be called for. For testing of an isolated Web page rather than an entire site, only a heuristic test would be performed. Local heuristic principles were developed, modeled on Jakob Nielsen's "Ten Usability Heuristics." (For the complete UVa Library heuristic principles, see: www.lib.virginia.edu/usability/heuristics.html)

When heuristic testing was called for, members of the Usability Group would perform the tests. The usability group developed guidelines for creating test questions, site owner questionnaires, and test log templates for use in conducting full usability tests. Test administration procedures were documented. (For all University of Virginia Library usability tests performed to date, see: www.lib.virginia.edu/usability/tests/; for the University of Virginia Library usability testing procedures, see: http://staff.lib.virginia.edu/usability/testing_procedures.htm)

The full testing process was relatively simple. Web design staff in the communications unit identified sites for full usability testing. In some cases, owners of sites not due for revision submitted their sites for testing because they saw room for improvement. The owner of each site was asked to fill out a site owner questionnaire to supply contextual information such as the mission, audience, and functions of the site. A set of 10 to 15 task-based test questions was developed by the usability group—no more than it would take an hour to test. Smaller sites had as few as seven questions. The questions required the testers to answer a question or perform a task without letting them know the information could be found on the site. The questions avoided the exact language used on the site to label the feature or function. The goal was that all questions should be written as "Is there?" or "Can you?" questions, not "Where is x in the site?" Full usability tests are available for review online (www.lib.virginia.edu/usability/tests/).

The goal was to test members of five categories of users representing undergraduates, graduates, faculty, library staff, and the public, if appropriate. Depending on the site, it might be tested with as few as three students of mixed type, three teaching faculty, and three library staff. Testers were solicited from the library staff through e-mail calls for participation. Faculty were solicited through personal requests from librarians. Students were most often employed by the library or were solicited by student library employees. Library employees remained on the clock for their tests. Students were paid $10 for their participation.

Card sorts were also sometimes used as part of the review of an existing library site to suggest revisions to a site's structure and labeling. The University of Virginia Library process was a closed card sort. Groups of no more than six to eight participants were given a stack of cards, one for each of the existing or suggested set of organizing categories and each single site page. Participants were asked to organize cards representing pages under the categories. The University of Virginia broke slightly from the usual practice by additionally allowing users to suggest new categories or new wording for category labeling. One or more groups, representing user constituencies, might be tested.

Members of the usability group administered all tests. Usability tests were administered with one tester, one facilitator, and one observer to record results on a paper log, logging steps taken by the tester with time elapsed in 15-second intervals. Tester's names were never recorded, only the category, such as faculty or graduate student. Test results were summarized, and a report was written by a member of the communications Web design staff for presentation to the site owner. The recommendations in the report were implemented whenever possible, but time and resources were not always available for site revisions in an environment where site maintenance was distributed. Sites were rarely re-tested after revisions have been made.

The University of Virginia Library developed a set of Balanced Scorecard metrics in 2001 for assessment purposes. A usability metric was implemented with the goal of testing 80 percent of all new or redesigned sites with either full usability or heuristic testing. For the first three years, the group either has met or narrowly missed its target.

2005 Review of Usability Procedures

In mid-2005, the usability group reviewed its procedures. This review was part of a library review of all processes covered by the Balanced Scorecard. Every year, the Balanced Scorecard metrics are reviewed for appropriateness in successfully assessing the target goals. The 2005 review was a major overhaul that covered the usefulness of every metric and the procedures used in capturing data for them. The Management Information Systems department coordinated the review, meeting with the units responsible for collecting data used in the annual compilations of results. Each metric was reviewed for appropriateness—does this metric really analyze data that helps us measure our success?—and methodology of data collection.

The site testing metric was previously grouped in the "Learning and Growth" category, meant to gauge how well the library was positioned to meet its goals in the future. The metric only measured that testing was performed at all, not whether a site was actually improved by the usability testing process. Usability testing and its metric are now part of the "Internal Process" category, reviewed in the context of how well the library's internal processes function to deliver library collections and services efficiently. The metric and usability testing procedures now better measure the outcomes of the usability testing process. The review produced a number of procedural changes.

The Underlying Principles and Guidelines Remain the Same

The criteria for identifying sites to be tested remain the same. Heuristic principles remain unchanged, as do test development guidelines and selection of categories of users.

The Process of Recording Test Results Must Change

Review of the observation and logging of test results showed that methods for recording tester activities, the level of detail recorded, and the consistency of time logging varied widely depending on who was doing the recording. To record tests more consistently, the library is switching from manual recording to the use of digital cameras and the Morae screen recording software.

The Definition of Success Must Change

What changed most drastically is the metric for success. Simply ensuring that sites were tested did not assure that testing brought about improvement in usability. Success is redefined as a documented improvement in the usability of a site.

Some Procedures Must Change to Better Measure Success

To better measure improvement, changes were needed in both the library's testing process and site development procedures. The old process was one in which a site was tested, the results reported to the site owner; changes were often (but not always) made; and updated sites were rarely re-tested. In the new process, test results are reported to the site owner, recommendations are reviewed with the Web design staff in the communications department, implementation of needed changes is required, and the site is always re-tested after it is revised.

The University of Virginia Library has not changed the guidelines for developing usability test tasks and the framing of questions. Instead, the library has identified an improved process for quantifying success. The revised metric is a comparison between the first and the second tests, where the percentage of right answers found by the tester in the first round of tests (regardless of the path they followed) is compared to the second round of tests where the same questions are used. Results are quantified by counting the number of right answers, and success measured through an improved percentage of right answers in re-testing.

While testing procedures have not changed, documentation of the procedures has been revised and expanded to include guidelines for all types of tests—heuristics, card sorts, and full usability tests—as well as for the development of tests and test follow-up (http://staff.lib.virginia.edu/usability/testing_ procedures.htm). The earlier version of this site focused solely on test administration.

Conclusion

This newly revised procedure also requires administrative and staff buy-in for changes in the library's site development process. Usability testing is now an integral part of the site development process, and library site owners must now take seriously the recommendations made based on usability testing. New documentation is under development to codify standards for setting up a University of Virginia Library site and identify the process for building a site that includes the involvement of (and accountability to) the Communications Department and the usability group.

Since implementing these procedural changes, the library underwent staffing changes that caused the usability testing program be put on hiatus. In 2007, this program was being revived and revitalized, and will now fully realize the goals identified in 2005. New testing equipment and the Morae software are in place, new staff is in place, and the library is newly committed to assessing its Web environment and improving the usability of online services for the community.

References

Nielsen, Jakob. 2005. "Ten Usability Heuristics." Available: www.useit.com/papers/heuristic/heuristic_list.html

Self, Jim. 2003. "From Values to Metrics: Implementation of the Balanced Scorecard in a University Library." *Performance Measurement and Metrics* 4, no. 2: 57–63.

117

Chapter 14

Usability Case Study: Wright State University

Vishwam Annam and Alison Aldrich

Context

Wright State University, named for aviation pioneers Orville and Wilbur Wright, is located in Dayton, Ohio. The university was founded in 1967. Today, nearly 17,000 students attend Wright State, which offers more than 100 undergraduate and 50 graduate and professional programs. Three libraries make up the University Libraries system. The Paul Laurence Dunbar Library is the main academic library on campus. The Fordham Health Sciences Library supports programs in medicine, nursing, psychology, and the biomedical sciences. The Lake Campus Library serves a branch campus in Celina, Ohio. Wright State University is a member of the OhioLINK (Ohio Library and Information Network) consortium. Wright State students, faculty, and staff have access to extensive print collections, as well as over 250 databases and 20,000 electronic journals.

Wright State University implemented SunGard SCT's Luminis as the campus portal in 2004. The portal, called WINGS, provides single sign-on access to university services such as course registration, grades, accounts, and campus activities. WINGS has tremendous potential to make the Wright State University community's work easier. It provides centralized access to systems and services that were previously dispersed on the university's Web site. WINGS administrators have the ability to push specific, relevant information to users based on their role in the university and field of study. This information appears in channels, which are small windows arranged on the portal's tabbed sections. Some channels are permanent parts of the WINGS interface, but other channels can be selected, deselected, and arranged by users to suit their own content preferences.

The university libraries created several optional channels for WINGS including channels for the catalog, course reserves, dictionary searching, and library news. These channels, which have been available to users since 2004, link to static pages on the libraries' Web site. In 2005, the University Libraries Web site received more than 850,000 different visits, but only 1.2 percent of these visitors came through the WINGS portal. The libraries are exploring ways to push more library content to WINGS to reduce the need for users to leave the portal interface to take advantage of library content and services.

The libraries would like to enable users to customize lists of resources (such as databases and journals) that they use most frequently, and would ultimately like library services such as requesting books, checking account status, and interlibrary loan to work under the single sign-on protocol for WINGS. Since the portal is designed to manage multiple accounts, the libraries are investigating different ways to create a customizable electronic library within WINGS. One example of a customizable electronic library system is MyLibrary. MyLibrary is open-source software originally developed by the Digital Library Initiatives department at North Carolina State University (Morgan, 2000). Since its initial release at NCSU in 1998, MyLibrary has been implemented at several other college and university libraries around the world.

Before implementing a customizable library for Wright State, the libraries conducted a small usability study to gauge their patrons' response to MyLibrary. The goals were to gather opinions from users about the library channels currently offered through WINGS and to assess the potential usefulness of a customizable electronic library product.

The Testing

Selecting Participants

According to Jakob Nielsen's frequently cited "rule of five" (Nielsen, 2000), 85 percent of a site's problems can be found with as few as five participants. However, when the audience for your product is composed of distinct groups of people, it is a good idea to select several participants from each group. In this study, the groups were undergraduate students, graduate students, faculty, and staff of Wright State University. Two undergraduate students and two graduate students were selected. Due to availability constraints, only one faculty member and one library reference staff member were included. Participants were chosen based on personal contacts, with an attempt made to find representatives from multiple fields of study. Tests were scheduled by e-mail or by phone. The team made note of the demographics (status, field of study) for each confirmed participant.

The Script

All tests used the same set of open-ended questions to capture clearly the different perspectives of the different audience groups. The script (Appendix 14A) consisted of three sections. In the first section, participants characterized their use of the library. In section two, participants described their use of WINGS and the library channels currently available within WINGS. In the final section, a guest login was used to demonstrate MyLibrary as implemented in Lehigh University's campus portal. Participants were asked to imagine how they might use customizable library services as a feature of WINGS.

Conducting the Usability Tests

The test monitor plays a crucial role in the success of any usability test. His or her role is to lead the participant through the test questions while being careful to not skew the results in any way. The monitor began each usability test by thanking the participant for volunteering, then reassuring the participant that the test was of the site, not of them.

The testing location was different for each participant, who selected the sites for comfort and convenience. The tests could be conducted from any computer with Internet access. In a more formal test, it is important to standardize the experience, conducting all tests at the same location, but in this case it was deemed that convenience was more important than formal methodology.

Findings

Results Summary

Participants' levels of experience with the libraries' Web site ranged from basic to advanced. The undergraduate students surveyed had used the site for course reserves and catalog searching but had little experience with article databases. Graduate students and faculty were more sophisticated in their use of the Web site. They generally reported bookmarking frequently used pages, such as the electronic journals list. The librarian did not bookmark pages because he was familiar enough with the site to navigate through it quickly as needed.

Of the six people surveyed, only one could be considered a regular WINGS user. This person, a graduate student, reported using WINGS about once a week, mainly for e-mail, the calendar, and the Academics tab. She had done some customization of her WINGS portal and was the only participant who knew about the library channels under the Academics tab. She supported leaving the tab as it was, with the library integrated with Academics. One undergraduate student had used the Course Studio function within WINGS.

Course Studio is an online course platform. It functions similarly to Blackboard or WebCT. Most participants used WINGS only rarely for e-mail, preferring an alternative URL for accessing Wright State e-mail via the Web. The library reference staff member was required to use WINGS to maintain his professional calendar and to access group messages and files, but was not satisfied with the efficiency of those processes.

Reaction to MyLibrary was mixed. One graduate student was very enthusiastic about the customization options and said that MyLibrary would increase her use of WINGS. Most other participants acknowledged that it was nice that customization options existed, but would not commit to saying MyLibrary was something they would use personally. The mechanics of customization seemed straightforward to the participants. However, the faculty member expressed a lack of confidence in his ability to choose the best customization options for himself. He worried about "missing something" and was pleased to hear that resources could be recommended for him by the subject liaison for his department. He also expressed reluctance to change his research habits unless MyLibrary made his work significantly easier.

The library reference staff member did not think students would be likely to use MyLibrary. The faculty member, on the other hand, commented that MyLibrary would probably get most of its use from people without ingrained research habits. Faculty and advanced graduate students typically have established library searching routines that work for them. If students learn to use MyLibrary as part of their introduction to library research, they might be more likely to continue using it as they progress through their academic careers.

Major Findings and Recommendations

- *Participants have not used the WINGS portal regularly.*
  WINGS is still fairly new, having first been released in 2004. As WINGS offers more services and a wider variety of content in future, more people are going to use it regularly.
- *Some participants could not find library services in WINGS.*
  Since library links in the portal are currently under the Academics tab, they usually go unnoticed. The links are only visible to users when they click on this tab. Since an expansion the library services available through WINGS is planned, the library could have its own tab, which would be visible from most pages within WINGS.
- *Most participants prefer having links to library resources by default rather than customizing their own lists.*
  Resources can be recommended for each patron group (undergraduate students, graduate students, staff, and faculty) by the subject liaisons for each academic department. Patrons, based on their demographics, will see links

that are already somewhat customized the first time they log in to the customizable library in WINGS.

Conclusion

This case study illustrates that usability testing can and should be done early on in the Web development process. By conducting just a few informal interviews, the libraries have gained a better understanding of how its patrons use the WINGS portal and what customized library services they would like to see in it.

Students, faculty, and staff have different library use patterns. The libraries are planning to develop a customizable library system in which the default display varies for students based on their majors or degree programs, and for faculty and staff based on department. This system also gives subject specialist librarians the ability to create views of the customizable library system with different sets of electronic resources, such as databases and electronic journals, depending on the status and department of the user. Since this system will be developed locally, it will be easier to maintain and troubleshoot. The WINGS portal is still in its introduction phase, but the libraries anticipate that more people will use it regularly in the future. The libraries are continuing with their plans to implement the customizable library within WINGS. As the project continues, they will conduct additional, more formal usability tests.

123

References

Morgan, Keith. 2000. "Pioneering Portals: MyLibrary@NCState." *Information Technology & Libraries* 19, no. 4: 191.

Nielsen, Jakob. 2000. "Why You Only Need to Test with Five Users." Alertbox (March 19). Available: www.useit.com/alertbox/20000319.html

Web Sites Tested

Wright Info, News and Group Services (WINGS)
http://wings.wright.edu

Wright State University Libraries
www.libraries.wright.edu

Lehigh University portal
http://portal.lehigh.edu

Appendix 14A: Script

Section 1:

1. Have you ever used the libraries' Web site before? If so, for what purpose?
2. How frequently do you use the libraries' Web site?
3. Do you bookmark the links you frequently use, or do you go through libraries' site every time?
4. If you had just the links you use collected in one place, instead of going through libraries' site every time to find them, would that help you?

Section 2:

In the second section, participants were asked to describe their use of WINGS and the library channels currently available within WINGS.

5. Have you ever used WINGS?
6. When was the first time you used WINGS? When was the last time you used it, and for what purpose?
7. How frequently do you use WINGS? What is your primary reason for using it?
8. What do you think is the main purpose of WINGS?
9. Did you know that the libraries offer some services through WINGS?
    • If yes, how did you come to know about these services?
    • If no, what services would you expect the libraries to offer through WINGS?
10. Where in WINGS would you expect to find these services?

Once users located the libraries' channels on the Academics tab of WINGS, they were given some time to look at the page.

11. Are you able to find most of the features that you normally use on the Libraries' site?

Section 3:

In this last section, a guest login was used to demonstrate MyLibrary as implemented in Lehigh University's campus portal. Participants were asked to imagine how they might use customizable library services as a feature of WINGS.

12. We are thinking about doing something like this . . . [Participants were shown MyLibrary as implemented through Lehigh's portal and given ample time to look at the site.]
13. What is your first impression of MyLibrary?
14. You can customize your electronic resources by following some simple steps. Would you like to try it?
15. What MyLibrary features you would like to see in our WINGS?
16. What group of people do you think would find MyLibrary most useful?
17. Would you use WINGS more often if something like MyLibrary were in place?
18. Do you have any other ideas or recommendations?

Chapter 15

Usability Case Study: Clinton-Macomb Public Library

Julianne Morian

Context

The Clinton-Macomb Public Library is a district library serving Clinton and Macomb Townships, which are located approximately 25 miles north of Detroit. Clinton Township is more established than Macomb Township due to its proximity to Detroit and its popularity as a suburban retreat in the 1960s and 1970s. Macomb Township has traditionally been a farming community, but in the 1990s, many farms were converted into subdivisions, now occupied by young professionals. This mix of young new families and seniors has created a diverse community of customers who frequent the library on a regular basis. While diverse in age, 74 percent of the population in Clinton Township and 90 percent of the population in Macomb Township are Caucasian. Eighty-four percent of adults have graduated from high school, and around 27 percent have obtained a bachelor's degree (U.S. Census Bureau, 2005).

The Challenge

In January 2002, the Clinton-Macomb Public Library's Web team decided to embark on a radical site redesign. The impetus for the redesign was the need to communicate information about the growing library system. With the passing of a new tax assessment in 1999, the library board had plans to open two new branches and a new main library building within four years. Clinton-Macomb Public Library needed a Web site that kept pace with the progressive culture of the library system and conveyed the professionalism and wealth of information within the organization.

Planning Phase

The Web team was comprised of four members: Three reference librarians with training in Web site design and usability assessment, and an assistant director with training in Web site design, programming, and usability. Web team members included Gretchen Krug, Branch Manager of the South Branch, Emily Kubash, Branch Manager of the North Branch, Juliane Morian, Head of Electronic Services, and Larry Neal, Director of the Clinton-Macomb Public Library.

The first step in the redesign was to identify the information gaps in the current site. The team researched other library Web sites to discover what information libraries made available on the Internet. The Web team also polled staff members to find the most commonly asked questions. The team compared its findings to the current iteration of the Web site and identified content that could be added.

The original Web site was designed and maintained by one person. It provided information such as hours and locations, a description of the library, a list of events and services at the library, and links to subscription databases, the online catalog, and recommended Web sites. It was a functional library Web site, but the team felt that if it could expand on its foundation, provide access to more online content, and create a logical architecture for navigating the site, the result would be a highly usable and noteworthy site.

Early in the project, the Web team members had an idea of what kind of second-level (or sub-pages) would be useful to the end user. The team felt there should be a homepage that displayed the most current information, then second-level pages that corresponded to the different library departments: Administration, Adult Nonfiction, Popular Materials (including adult fiction and audio-visuals), Children's Services, Teen Services, and Outreach. There was a desire to provide a colorful Web site featuring plenty of pictures, and a consistent style with similar fonts, bullets, spacing, and layout.

The team met on a monthly basis, with smaller meetings scheduled in between if necessary. The first big project was to create a layout that would be used as the starting design. Rather than design the proposed layout as a group, the team used individual time to brainstorm and formulate a layout, adopting the theory that some of the best designs are conceived at the individual level. Each team member interpreted his or her desire for color, pictures, and style in a slightly different way. Some individuals drew a design on paper while others used computer software to render a proposed layout. The designs that had the most appeal used color and graphics; those that were text-heavy did not elicit as much enthusiasm. Team members took turns commenting on each design, occasionally offering constructive criticism, but more often than not identifying strong elements on each of the proposed design that they liked the most. Ultimately, one design generated unanimous appeal. The team focused on that design and integrated elements from the other designs so that the final layout was collaborative and inclusive.

One of the significant design elements that first emerged in the planning phase of the project was the navigation bar. As a group, the team decided to place the navigation pane on the left side of the interface. The team identified nine categories: "About us," "Catalog," "Databases," "Events," "Youth," "Fiction titles," "Local links," "Talk to us," and "Site index." These categories reflected the mission of the reference desk (where team members provide readers advisory and reference service for children and adults) and the teams' experience at the information desk, where the circulation staff answers questions regarding the library system, policies, contact information, and community information. The goal of creating the nine categories was to make the new site more broad than deep. Building on principles in Louis Rosenfeld and Peter Morville's book *Information Architecture for the World Wide Web* (1998), the team felt it should "lean towards a broad and shallow rather than deep and narrow hierarchy."

The team had an idea of the information they wanted to place in each category but needed to visualize it. One member volunteered to create a wireframe of the site to let the team see how some of the information would be organized. A wireframe is a design on paper that categorizes information according to how it will be displayed on a Web page (see Figure 15.1). In this case, the wireframe was designed using Microsoft Word and text boxes, which was low-tech and easy for anyone to modify. Boxes were used to represent the various clusters of information on a page, including the proposed title of the page at the top and a list of the content below.

A second team member used Microsoft Excel to map out a site architecture. Similar to a wireframe, this architecture listed the title of the page in a cell and used lines to represent the information on the various sublevels (see Figure 15.2). This architecture was very useful when dividing up the task of actually creating the pages and was used to mark each page as complete after internal quality-assurance testing.

Finally, a third member of the team created a Web style guide (see Figure 15.3), which identified the header font, paragraph font, style of bullets, the spacing requirements (such as not leaving a blank line between a heading and a paragraph) and how to display time and date information (such as A.M. or AM in small capitals). The style guide also included reference material such as the dimensions of the design area and the hex value for the color palette (see Figure 15.4).

127

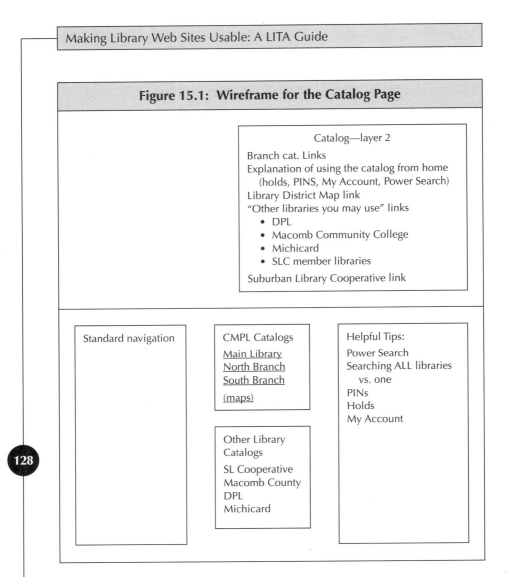

Figure 15.1: Wireframe for the Catalog Page

Catalog—layer 2
Branch cat. Links
Explanation of using the catalog from home
(holds, PINS, My Account, Power Search)
Library District Map link
"Other libraries you may use" links
- DPL
- Macomb Community College
- Michicard
- SLC member libraries
Suburban Library Cooperative link

Standard navigation

CMPL Catalogs
Main Library
North Branch
South Branch

(maps)

Other Library
Catalogs
SL Cooperative
Macomb County
DPL
Michicard

Helpful Tips:
Power Search
Searching ALL libraries
vs. one
PINs
Holds
My Account

User Testing

At this stage in the design process, the team had spent about seven months planning and mocking up the site in various iterations. The team felt confident the proposed layout and site architecture was on target, but had not tested it beyond the four-member group. The team decided that, before creating the pages in HTML, the design should be tested on real users to get their feedback on how well the navigation worked for them. The team also wanted to be sure the information logically belonged to the category to which it had been assigned.

Working from the wireframes, one member entered all the information elements into cells in Microsoft Excel and expanded the cells to the size of an

Figure 15.2: Spreadsheet of Site Architecture

Homepage			
	LibraryTour		
Library			
	HoursLocation		
	PhoneDirectory		
	About Us		
		MainBranch	
		NorthBranch	
		SouthBranch	
		BoardofTrustees	
	DirectorWelcome		
		Director'sResume	
	Employment		
		Open Positions	
		Closed Positions	
		EmploymentApp	
	SupportLibrary		
		LibraryVolunteers	
			VolunteerApplicationForm
		Friends	
			FriendsApplicationForm
		DonationsContributions	
	Cards		
		LibraryCardApplicationForm	
	MaterialsLoansPeriodsFines		
	PickUpReturnRenew		
	LibraryTips		
	OtherLibraries		

index card. The file was printed on card stock, and each information element was cut out. There were more than 200 information elements (or cards).

One member e-mailed the staff and asked for volunteers to participate in the card sorting exercise. Four staff members responded, and the Web team member scheduled one-hour sessions. In each card sorting session, the volunteer staff member was instructed to read through each of the cards and then place them into logical groups. When finished, they were asked to name the groups they created. Two of the volunteer staff members created more than 20 categories, and two created fewer than 10.

Despite the difference in the number of categories created, the staff members grouped the information fairly consistently. Also, the team decided that some of the categories in the 20-plus category groups could be combined with other categories. An example of this was the category "Volunteer and Donation Information." Logically, this could exist as its own category, but it could also be included in the "Library Information" category. So the Web team analyzed the results from the card sorting exercise and made any necessary changes to the site architecture.

In addition to card sorting exercises, the Web team set up six usability tests in which volunteer staff members interacted with a mocked-up version of the site and attempted to navigate to information. A Web team member designed a

---

Figure 15.3: Web Style Guide

Web Site Annotations
Annotations should include 2-3 clear, concise, accurate sentences that describe the content of the site. Comments should focus on specific aspects of the site ("this page offers a prehistoric timeline") as opposed to vague assertions ("this site has information about dinosaurs").

Web Site Annotations—Titles
Web site titles should be entered consistently. When developing a Web site title, think about how it corresponds to what you expect to see on the site. Capitalize each significant word as you would a book title. For example, This Great Web Site.

Web Site Headers
Headers, the title text next to the colored squares, are Trebuchet, 12 point, bold font.

Web Site Text
General text, any information under the headers, follow Georgia, 12 point, normal font.

Back to the Top Text
Long blocks of text may be broken up with "Back to the top" in Trebuchet, 10 point, normal font.

Squares & Headers
There is one space between a colored square and the beginning of the header text.

Drop-Down Menus
Drop down menus use Georgia, 12 point, normal font.

Breadcrumbs
Breadcrumbs are used when a page is two or more layers away from a main Web page. Breadcrumbs indicate a way to back up through previously viewed pages. For instance: Library > Support the Library > Library Volunteers

Breadcrumbs text are Georgia, 10 point, normal font. Arrows are Arial, 8 point, normal font. There is one full carriage return after the breadcrumb.

Download Required
Some documents may require the use of free viewing software. In these instances we will indicate this requirement and the file's size.

An example of the format followed is: (file size 100K—Adobe Acrobat required). This is Georgia, 10 point, normal font. The text name of the required software should be hyperlinked to the page with instructions on how to download said software.

Use of Buttons
Use a button (insert pic example) rather than a plain text link when linking to a form. A good example is the button that links to the Friends membership form.

(Cont'd.)

Figure 15.3: Web Style Guide *(Continued)*

Site Index

Header alphabet letters follow Trebuchet, 12 point, bold font.

Text links are Georgia, 12 point, normal font.

Kids and Teens links are indicated by placing (Kids) or (Teens) one space after the text link. For example, Book List Links (Teens).

---

usability script that included 10 tasks (see Appendix 15A) with questions ranging from "Where can you find information about kids' story times?" to "Can you find a medical-oriented database?"

The usability tests provided valuable information about some of the labels the Web team had applied to the categories. For instance, databases were located under a navigation button titled "eResources." Some of the volunteer

---

Figure 15.4: Web File Structure Procedures

CMPL Web Site File Structure Procedures

Directories:

1. Each directory address will end with default.htm or default.asp depending on the directories' contents.

Creating File Names:

1. Title should reflect file contents.
2. Upper and lower case letters are allowed.
3. Do not use spaces or underscores when naming files.

Saving Web Images:

1. Images relevant to the site as a whole will be stored in the Images directory.
2. Images directory will include folders for each of the other directories.
3. Within each directory's folder there will be a sub-folder for ImagesPermanent and a sub-folder for ImagesTemporary.
4. File name words that are common across directories should have other specific keywords added to the file name.
   Example: images/kids/line   vs.   images/kids/orangeline
5. Sub-directories will be created at the discretion of the Web site maintainer, but should not be overused.
6. Image sizes should not exceed...???
7. Image file names will follow a specific format of: yearmonthdaytitle.
   For example an image of George Washington could have a file name of: 20020421GeorgeWashington
   Here, year=2002, month=04, day=21, and title=George Washington.

testers experienced confusion when trying to find a database because they were looking for the word "database" and did not know what "eResources" referred to. The team did not know if this test data was reliable, since librarians have extensive knowledge about what a database is, yet reference desk interactions suggested that customers were not familiar with the word "database." Ultimately, the team decided that either label choice, "databases" or "eResources," was equally ambiguous for the average user but that eResources was a less intimidating word choice than databases. As a result of usability testing, the team also changed "Talk to Us" to "Contact Us" since that was a more familiar convention for Web users and encompassed multiple methods of communication. Finally, the team settled on the label "Good Reads" for the page that provided readers advisory. The group considered a variety of labels for this page to avoid being format-specific ("Good Words," "Good Finds," "Nice Picks"), but due to space constraints and ambiguous alternatives, the Web team decided that "Good Reads" was an acceptable title for information on readers advisory.

The team analyzed the feedback gathered in the usability tests and identified over 30 modifications they could implement to make the Web site more intuitive. These included using consistent terminology (e.g., kids, children, youth, teens); modifying headers to be more precise (e.g., changing "Web Links" to "Popular Search Sites"), and reordering the layout to maximize screen space.

Redesign Phase

At this stage of the project, the Web team divided up the work of coding the new pages and started to create a new site. Each Web team member took charge of three subcategories.

Over a five-week period, the Web team designed the graphic elements and coded the pages. The site contained the following category labels: Library, Catalog, Events, eResources, Kids, Teens, Good Reads, Community, Contact Us, and Find It. Each category was assigned a different color. The assigned color appeared as the user moused over the first-level navigation button and appeared within elements on the page once the user clicked into that category.

Before launching the site, the team conducted quality assurance by testing each link on every page.

Findings

On the whole, the Clinton-Macomb Public Library is very proud of its Web site, and the Web team feels it meets the needs of online users. But in retrospect, there are a number of things the Web team could have done differently to create an even better Web site. The team should have:

- used non-staff users in the testing
- introduced the card sorting exercise earlier in the design phase
- used fewer elements in the card-sorting exercises
- built in one practice round for user testing

Perhaps because the team was young and lacked experience, they did not feel confident approaching customers and asking them to assist with formal user testing of the site. Staff volunteers gave very useful information, but in many instances they were already familiar with the librarian lingo that sometimes can confuse a real user.

The team also learned that if they had introduced the card sorting exercise earlier in the design phase, they could have incorporated more intuitive labels earlier in the design process. By the time the Web team conducted card sorting exercises, the team had already developed the proposed layout. That meant the team knew what kind of navigation buttons they wanted to appear on the site, but those navigation buttons had fixed widths. The team learned in the card sorting exercise that, in some instances, a longer label might have been better than the one chosen, but using that new label would have distorted the consistent look of the site, resulting in a wider button or a smaller font on the button. An example of this was the category called "Community." Originally, this was conceived as a page devoted to local information. "Community" is not a very illustrative label because it is too vague. A volunteer tester suggested "Local Links" as an alternative label, but that was outside the width allowance. The team made the decision not to compromise all the work put into the layout and rather accepted the responsibility of teaching users what information lay behind the navigation element. A better approach would have been to introduce card sorting exercises before the categories were settled on and to allow users to give feedback and collaborate on the titles of the categories.

The team discovered that asking volunteer testers to sort through 200-plus cards, place them in categories, and name the categories in less than one hour was quite ambitious. In some instances, volunteers were unable to sort through all the cards thoroughly, sometimes resulting in skewed tests in which some categories were fleshed out with logical information elements but other categories were bare, simply because the volunteer ran out of time. In retrospect, the cards should have been created with very broad information elements. Instead of 200 cards, reducing the number of cards to 120 or fewer would have been much better for a 60-minute session.

Finally, it would have been better to make the first user test a practice round for the facilitator. Obtaining valid results from user testing requires the use of a consistent script, so that when the team evaluates how each volunteer

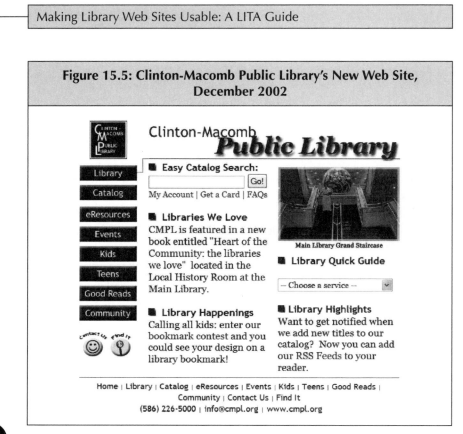

Figure 15.5: Clinton-Macomb Public Library's New Web Site, December 2002

reacted to a test question, the team knows the facilitator presented it the same way each time. After conducting the first usability test, the facilitator decided to tweak some of the questions for the subsequent volunteers. Tweaking the questions was perfectly acceptable, but the team should have removed the feedback from the practice round.

Conclusion

Clinton-Macomb Public Library proudly launched its new Web site in December 2002 (see Figure 15.5).

The Web team was committed to conducting some usability analysis before taking the site live. In hindsight, the team could have improved results by focusing more on the target audience and integrating user testing earlier in the process. Since the Web team was comprised of reference librarians, the team has benefited from watching users interact with the site. There have been many adjustments and improvements over the years. The library has added a calendar system for the events page, and a content management system for recommended Web links and forms have provided a consistent method for users to give feedback (see Figure 15.6). The Clinton-Macomb Public Library is gearing up for

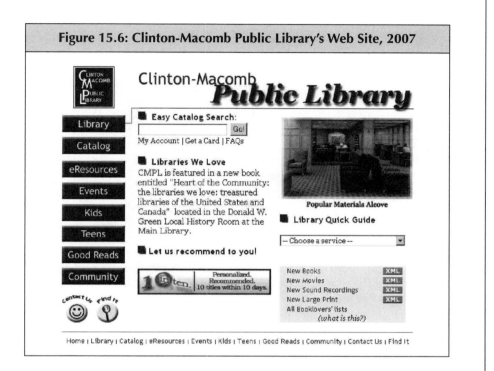

Figure 15.6: Clinton-Macomb Public Library's Web Site, 2007

a second redesign of the site and will undoubtedly incorporate the lessons learned from the first redesign.

135

References

Rosenfeld, Louis, and Peter Morville. 1998. *Information Architecture for the World Wide Web*. Sebastopol, CA: O'Reilly & Associates.

U.S. Census Bureau. 2005. "2005 American Community Survey Data Profile." Available: http://factfinder.census.gov (accessed December 12, 2006).

Appendix 15A: User Testing Script

☑ Thank you for participating in our user-testing session. I will be reading from my notes today to make sure that I remain consistent.

☑ We will be evaluating a new Web site for the Clinton-Macomb Public library. As you may know, the Clinton-Macomb Public Library is comprised of three branches, a temporary Main branch, a South branch, and a North branch.

☑ Today we want to get feedback on how well the new site works for you. We are going to ask you to complete 10 tasks.

☑ While you are interacting with the Web site, it is most beneficial to us if you think out loud. Thinking out loud can consist of any thoughts you have about the site or the experience such as, "I didn't expect this . . ." or "I think I'll try this link next . . ." and so on . . .

☑ The proposed new site is largely in "mock-up" form, meaning few, if any, of the blue hyperlinks actually work. In the instances where you want to click on a blue link but cannot, please verbally tell us that you want to click on that link.

☑ If you encounter challenges when trying to complete the task, I cannot assist you to your goal. It is precisely these challenges that we are trying to identify and eradicate, so it is important for me to watch your actions and listen to your thought processes as you work through these tasks, regardless of difficulty.

☑ During this session, I will be taking notes. At times I may prompt you for more information about a choice you made or a comment you stated. At the end of each task you will have an opportunity to give me feedback.

☑ Do you have any questions before we begin?

Questions for the User:

1. Where can you find information about kids' story times?
2. Can you find an explanation of how to use the catalog?
3. Does the library have any book club activities?
4. Your 4th grader has a science experiment project, where would you go to find this kind of information?
5. Find two ways to locate a list of phone numbers for the CMPL libraries—each time start from the homepage.
6. Please find information on daycare services at the Clinton-Macomb Public Library.
7. Using this Web site, find out if there is a Senior Services Department in Clinton or Macomb Township.
8. How can you make suggestions or comments about the site?
9. Can you find a medical-oriented database?
10. Your teen is interested in a career in nursing, where would you go to find that kind of information?

Chapter 16

Usability Case Study: The MITRE Corporation

Stacy Surla

Context

The MITRE Corporation is an organization of knowledge workers. Around 6,000 scientists, engineers, and specialists serve on a range of engineering and IT projects for U.S. government sponsor agencies. The corporate Information Services (IS) department provides custom knowledge management services to support these staff. It also arranges access to internal and external publications and other analytic resources. MITRE's workforce is widely distributed throughout the United States and across the globe. A large proportion of the staff works remotely at least part of the time or is based at a site other than one of the two main campuses. The corporate intranet is therefore a main source for technical information and access to the expertise of colleagues and is a key means for collaboration, sharing, and publishing within MITRE.

The IS Web collection consists of a homepage, about 20 subsites, and over 5,300 individual pages and files. Consistency is provided via a shared masthead and navigation scheme. One of the subsites provides access to the digital libraries themselves, which comprise hundreds of electronic databases, full-text journals, books, and other external digital library resources. Access to external resources is facilitated by browse views generated from a database. There are also many internal resources, including half a dozen catalogs of MITRE-produced reports, blogs, discussion lists, Microsoft SharePoint document repository and team collaboration sites, and other sources of internal knowledge.

However, the IS Web collection (Figure 16.1) reflects a piecemeal approach that is straining to accommodate growth in the number and types of its assets, and is in danger of falling behind the evolving direction of the corporate intranet. The current collection has inconsistent navigation, poor

137

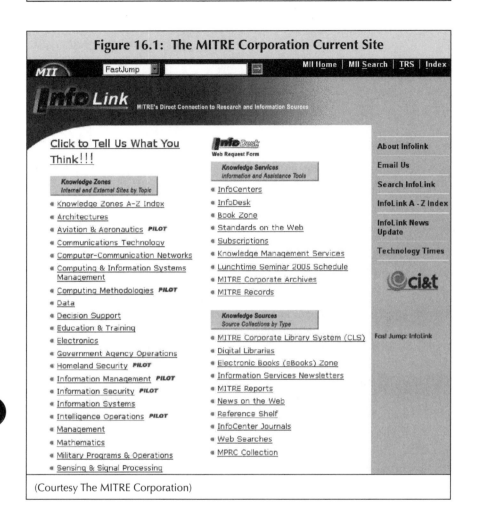

Figure 16.1: The MITRE Corporation Current Site

(Courtesy The MITRE Corporation)

wayfinding cues, a complicated information organization, a crowded and confusing visual design, and a fair amount of outdated information. The collection is not tailored for key audiences or the tasks they are trying to fulfill, but is based on the IS department's team structure (current and past). Each part of the collection is an individual "best solution" but does not reflect a holistic approach to delivering services. As a result, the collection does not meet user needs or expectations for accessibility and self-service. It is time-consuming to use and maintain and difficult to scale. It does not directly integrate with information access across the enterprise. In short, a significant proportion of MITRE staff does not know where to go to access information services. Information is hard to find and the gems are hidden.

The Redesign of the MITRE Digital Library

The redesign of the IS collection was undertaken to make information resources easier to find and use, and make the collection scalable and easier to maintain. A cross-disciplinary team was assembled. This team included a project manager, subject matter experts, information architects, a visual designer, user-centered design advisors, and developers. The project was being implemented in a series of self-contained phases. This approach helped keep the project in scope while staging important advanced functions on an agreed-upon future timeline.

Phase I (four months) focused on getting the lay of the land. This involved discovering the size and nature of the current IS collection, understanding the user base, learning the problems of the current site, and soliciting stakeholder ideas and visions for the collection.

In January 2007, the project was in Phase II (eight months). This work was concentrating on developing an information architecture (IA) and visual design for the new IS collection, focusing on the digital libraries subsite, and bringing selected applications into alignment with the new navigation and visual design.

Future phases will address unifying the search and browse experience across multiple catalogs, adding richer interactivity such as faceted browse and customized situational awareness feeds, integrating social tagging with structured taxonomies, and making digital library assets easier to reach from the enterprise search and browse navigation.

Most of the problems being addressed by the redesign are not unique to library Web sites. The user-centered practices followed in developing the information architecture for the IS collection can be applied to any complex information space. However, several issues have emerged that do pertain specifically to digital libraries, including designing good interfaces for lists and crafting the user experience when target objects lie outside the digital library. These special challenges will be discussed in more detail following a high-level review of the project approach and user-centered design tasks.

User-Centered Design

User-centered design approaches fit particularly well into certain project tasks. This approach nonetheless required deliberate attention at times to keep a sharp focus on the user, particularly during tasks that could be carried out more swiftly without bringing the user into the equation. One helpful tactic was to use methodologies new to the team, including user-centered requirements gathering, persona development, competitive analysis, and user testing via card sorting and paper prototyping. While accomplishing the specific goals for which they were designed, these methodologies also engaged the team in thinking about Web development in new ways.

User-Centered Requirements Gathering

The first major task was to figure out exactly who uses the information services and why. The objective was to change the answer from "all of MITRE" to some discrete number of audience types and task scenarios. The team talked to frontline IS staff to determine who their users are, what tasks they are carrying out, and what content they are looking for. Although the goal was to redesign the Web collection and not the IS workflow, the team explicitly asked for details about the offline as well as online means by which customers are served. The team also conducted interviews with frequent users of IS and asked them about their work practices and information-gathering routines in general, as well as their use of IS services in particular. The result was an audience matrix with a dozen user types and representative tasks (see Figure 16.2).

Next, visual, descriptive documents called "personas" were developed for key audience types. Personas make designers' assumptions about target audiences more explicit and help concentrate decision making on targeted user needs, attributes, and scenarios. However, their greatest value may be in providing a shared basis for communication in a cross-disciplinary team. Personas encapsulate information from interviews, market research, ethnographic research, usability tests, and other sources and can convey decisions about key user groups in a way that is easy to grasp and share. More common in product design and marketing (see Alan Cooper's discussion of personas at: www.cooper.com/insights/journal_of_design/articles/the_origin_of_personas_1.html), they are beginning to be used in software and Web site design. The persona development process helped refine the list to four key types: Technical/ professional staff, information analyst, administrative assistant, and new employee.

While conducting the audience tasks, the team also carried out an asset inventory (see Figure 16.3). This lists major and minor pages, links, applications, navigation elements, and other features of a collection in a spreadsheet format that is useful for getting a handle on a Web site's size and nature. It is also the foundation for later work. When overlaid, for instance, with an audience matrix, the asset inventory helps identify gaps in content, audience coverage, and navigation. When preparing content for the new site, it provides a baseline of existing content.

One particularly important—and often very challenging—step in any IT project is to figure out which applications, Web sites, utilities and other systems will interact with the new one. From a purely technical point of view, it is necessary to identify these dependent and related systems so they can be integrated with your own system. A user-centered process takes this need one step further, since user-centered design is deeply concerned with knowing where users will come into contact with any other systems. The designers need to understand the potential for a more difficult or an enhanced user experience at each turn, so they can design the Web interactions accordingly. The key systems for the IS collection redesign include the customer relationship management (CRM) system, search, the database of external digital libraries, internal catalogs on SIRSI and other platforms, Microsoft SharePoint, and a newly acquired license for journal search and retrieval from a company called Serials Solutions. For each system, the team must frame user-centered questions for both technical staff and users. The answers help the team develop blueprints for a Web site that serves user needs and yet is also technically feasible. For instance, at MITRE, users currently can contact IS staff with questions and requests using a Web form that is integrated with a CRM system. This happens to be the same system used by the help desk to manage help request tickets. The IS form does not share the IS collection look and feel, but instead looks just like the help desk form. The team's questions for IT staff, Information Services staff, and users included: "Are users disoriented by the form, and if so, are they less likely to ask for help because of that?" "Do Information Services staff still want to use the form as a channel for communication?" "Can the IT staff change the navigation, visuals, and layout of the form so it will match the rest of the Information Services site?" and "Can this be done within the scheduled timeframe for our project?" (The answers to these questions all happened to be yes.)

The team also carried out a competitive analysis, a review of other external and internal Web sites, navigation schemes, and Web services that provide knowledge and digital library services or organize large amounts of customer-facing content in effective ways. This analysis can be quite sophisticated, but in this case it consisted of a set of screenshots of Web sites with overlaid notes about each site. Even when one is not engaged in a competition to capture market share, a competitive analysis can be quite useful. It helped the team design with an awareness of the visual design and navigation of related sites in its own organization, and also inspired the team to learn from the best practices of others (and to try to go one better). It is important, however, to resist the temptation to copy visual designs and layouts from other sites. Instead, the team used this as an occasion to analyze other sites to figure out how they solved particular information organization problems.

Wireframe the Solutions

Armed with in-depth information gleaned through these and other tasks, the next step was to devise trial solutions and then test and refine them until a set of working blueprints was developed. The team followed an iterative process, which allowed several cycles of engagement among decision makers, users, and members of the team. What the team was explicitly trying to avoid was

Figure 16.2: Audience Matrix		
InfoLink Update		**v.1.0 :: Team :: 12/05/05**
User Role	**Priority**	**Description**
Role name	[primary, secondary, or tertiary]	[General description of role and customer characteristics]
Project leader	primary	Been at MITRE 5 years, works with sponsor and team, project focused, manages people, uses the phone mostly
Engineer	primary	New to MITRE but just out of grad school and familiar with the concept of digital libraries and computer savvy to the point of overload, not familiar with MITRE processes. Feels overwhelmed and a little lost.
Engineer, associate manager	primary	Manager that delegates research and the details of the job, been at MITRE 15 years and hasn't kept up with changes in technology. Uses phone or e-mail, relies on an immediate response so they ask the first person they see.
Admin staff	primary	Supports 10 staff and 4 managers. Makes travel plans, schedules, sets up VTCs, conferences, manages office supplies, coordinates office moves
Information intelligence analyst	secondary	At MITRE 4 years, softshells from task to task, needs to learn new information resources. Mostly uses e-mail or phone, telecommutes or works at sponsor site. Sticks with old, comfortable people resources and standards.
Engineer, lead	tertiary	Sole job is to keep abreast of standards such as Tax XML and attend international standards meetings related to this standard. Travels a lot. Computer savvy, good at PowerPoint. Uses contacts from previous jobs. At MITRE 5 years, higher education.
Information Analysts, Knowledge Services	primary	Conduct and provide research, current awareness, MLS, produce/publish newsletters, site briefings
		(Columns continue)

142

Figure 16.2: Audience Matrix *(Columns Continued)*

Representatives	User Tasks	Team Services
[Names of people in this group]	[What people in this category are doing when they use your services]	[Specific services they use. Describe, or use labels from Services Matrix]
Mary	About to give a briefing and needs an immediate fact for a chart	Call Infodesk or asks around, checks digital libraries or Internet, attends and holds TEMS, needs help with organization of his materials
John (as suggested by Rose)	Wants to understand industry best practices and find MITRE experts working the same type of project, as well as case studies and other mediated research	Google expert finder, knowledge services, Infodesk
Ask Infodesk for someone	Weekly sponsor meetings, oversight of contractor work which is highly technical	Walks into the library, attends TEMS
Candy, Alex	Ordering journals, research, keeps schedules of corporate papers and records retention	Uses linfolink for reference research, check with Gina or Tea about records
Myrna	Leads new tasks, attends working group meetings and TEMS, conducts research	Uses listservs, librarians list, use community share sites, records management repositories
Frank, James	Attends international standards meetings, briefs at the meetings such as OASIS, and briefs MITRE sponsors and employees, writes formal deliverables and documentation	Research from KM Services, uses the Internet and standards discussion groups. Attends working groups in person or on phone.
Lisa, Anna	Providing information and custom KM services to clients	Various offerings of Information Services (see services matrix)

(Table continues)

143

Figure 16.2: Audience Matrix *(Continued)*

InfoLink Update   v.1.0 :: Team :: 12/05/05

User Role	Priority	Description
Role name	[primary, secondary, or tertiary]	[General description of role and customer characteristics]
Site Engineer	secondary	Works directly with sponsor. Uses e-mail and phone. Possibly no MII access, military background and domain experts
MTP (MSR or MOIE)	secondary	Limited or finite budget from mitre. Research oriented.
Officers or Board members	tertiary	Very high-level, work is sporadic in nature?
CCKS writers and photographers	secondary	What's their profile?
Technical Manager, principle staff	primary	PhD, MITRE for 10 years, co-principle investigator, provides classified analytic support for government analysts, focusing on a particular area, field expert

Questions being answered by the Audience Matrix
Who are the users?
What tasks do they carry out on the site?
What content are they looking for?

Also see/create
Services Matrix for this task

design behind a dark curtain, unveiled with a flourish as a highly polished *fait accompli*. Rather, design work should be open and participatory, with products at each step that are easy to change. At the same time, the attention of clients and colleagues is a precious resource and must not be squandered, so work products should clearly communicate which elements are up for discussion, revision, or approval.

Figure 16.2: Audience Matrix *(Columns Continued)*		
Representatives	**User Tasks**	**Team Services**
[Names of people in this group]	[What people in this category are doing when they use your services]	[Specific services they use. Describe, or use labels from Services Matrix]
Dorothy	Working closely with sponsor attending meetings, doing research, finding best practices, and oversight	Relies on liaison from KMS for custom research, Infodesk for articles
Petra, Steve	Doing research and testing	TBD
Doris, Trish	Business development work, writing articles, looking for testimony and facts	Needs custom KM research and current awareness
Darna, Max	Write articles and take photos for MITRE publications, MII and external audiences.	Research or photo requests on a topic or about MITRE work, uses Infodesk and digital libraries, corporate archives
Fulvio	Researching various intel sources, produces own newsletters	Subscribes to alerts or newsletters from InfoServices, reads news papers and periodicals, uses RSS feeds
(Courtesy The MITRE Corporation)		

145

Low-fidelity prototypes are important in the early stages of the design process. Sketches on napkins are good examples (if they make sense and are large enough for everyone to see). Wireframe diagrams, paper prototypes, mind maps, storyboards, index cards bearing navigation labels, workflow diagrams, and even rough HTML pages can all be effective low-fidelity prototypes. As various information organization and design decisions are made, the

Figure 16.3: Asset Inventory

Library   00/00/2007

Asset ID	Item Num	Level 0 Link Name	Level 1 Link Name	Level 2 Link Name	Level 3 Link Name
		Site Location			
MN.11.00	1		Library Site		
		Header Navigation—Toolbar 1			
MN.00	2	Intranet Home			
		Multipart Search Interface			
AN.01	5	Global Phonebook			
AN.04	6	Global Dashboard			
AN.05	9	Global Timesheet			
MN.19	10	Library Sitemap			
		Header Navigation—Right Nav and Toolbar 2			
MN.11.01	11			About Library Site	
EO.11.01	26				Email Us
MN.11.01.02	27				Search Library Site
MN.11.01.03	28				Library Size A-Z Index
MN.11.01.04	29				Library Site News
		Content Area Navigation			
AO.04.02	33				Request Form
MN11.04	58			Library Subsection 1	
AN.03	59	Global Search			
EO.11.01	60				Email Us
MN.11.00	61		Library Site [image]		
MN.11.05	62			Library Subsection 2	
MN.11.06	81			Library Subsection 3	
MN.11.05	126			Subscriptions	
MN.11.12	200			Digital Libraries	
MN.11.13	364			Electronic Books	
MN11.14	379			Newsletters	

(Columns continue)

Figure 16.3: Asset Inventory *(Columns Continued)*

URL	Notes
http://intranet/Library/index.html	
http://intranet/index.html	
http://intranet/phonebook	
http://intranet/dashboard	Maintained by Group A
http://intranet/timesheet	
http://intranet/Library/alphabetical_index/	
http://intranet/Library/about	
library@company.com	
http://intranet/Library/focussearch	.
http://intranet/Library/azindex.html	
http://intranet/Library/news_update.html	
http://server/jsp	This is on the IT department site—confusing
http://intranet/Library/section1	
http://intranet/Library/index.html	
library@company.com	
http://intranet/Library/index.html	
http://intranet/Library/section2	
http://intranet/Library/section 3	
http://intranet/Library/section1	This just leads back to Library Subsection 1
http://intranet/Library/digital_libraries/index/shtml	Navigation through collection is complicated
http://intranet/Library/ebooks.html	
http://intranet/Library/newsletters	
	(Table continues)

Figure 16.3: Asset Inventory *(Continued)*

Library   00/00/2007

Asset ID	Item Num	Level 0 Link Name	Level 1 Link Name	Level 2 Link Name	Level 3 Link Name
		Content Area Navigation (Continued)			
MN.11.15	402			Reports	
MN.11.16	426			News	
MN.11.17	435			Reference Shelf	
				Journals	
		Footer Navigation			
	502			Mail to library@company.com	
		Needed Links NOT On InfoLink			
		[add any missing links here]			

(Courtesy The MITRE Corporation)

148

prototypes can become more detailed or higher-fidelity. The key is to use tools the team is comfortable with and that make it easier to brainstorm, test, refine, and communicate solutions for all aspects of the Web site design.

The team started with several high-level concepts for the IS collection and created wireframe diagrams for each of these (see Figure 16.4). Wireframes sketch out key pages, site maps, and navigation flows, and can also contain notes pointing out the logic that runs through the design and how the proposed information architecture fulfills the requirements.

After reviewing the annotated wireframes with appropriate decision makers, the team settled on self-service and task-based organization as the organizing principles for the new IS collection.

A round of user testing took place after a sufficient number of tentative decisions had been made about site organization. The wireframe diagrams for proposed top sections were stripped of their comments and used as paper prototypes. Card sorting exercises were also carried out to identify users' expectations regarding terminology and site organization. The team identified moderate and heavy users of the current IS collection who fit the profiles of the key user groups. They provided insights that enabled the team to nail down several aspects of the design. They also posed new questions that led

Figure 16.3: Asset Inventory *(Columns Continued)*	
URL	**Notes**
http://intranet/Library/reports.html	
http://intranet/Library/enews.html	links to newspapers, wires, news feeds
http://intranet/Library/reference.html	links to reference books
http://intranet/Library/journals.html	

back to the drawing board on some other key issues—for instance, whether the homepage of the new collection should contain a lot of rich content or would be better as a streamlined entry page. Higher-fidelity visual designs were developed to help make final decisions on page layout (see Figure 16.5).

Digital Library-Specific Challenges

There are a number of interesting issues with the digital library part of the project. These can perhaps be reduced to two key challenges: Providing list interfaces that present the right types and amount of information, and crafting the user experience when target objects lie outside the digital library.

Lists: The Right Information the Right Way

Digital library listings follow various models. Some look like Google results pages. Some display large amounts of information and resemble card catalogs. Others are merely bulleted lists or tables. In each case, the person designing the list interface has to select which attributes to display for each information object. This should not be primarily a technological decision ("these fields are available in the database, so let's show those"), nor even a cultural one ("we're used to seeing bulleted lists, so we'll do this the same way"), but

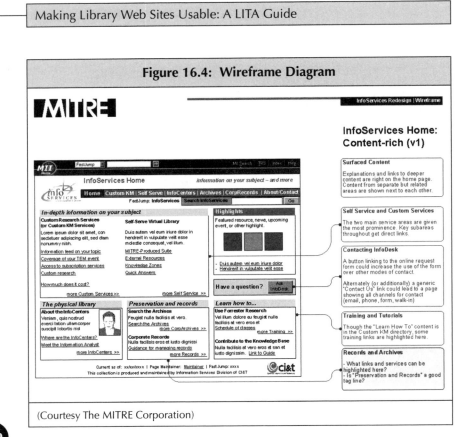

Figure 16.4: Wireframe Diagram

(Courtesy The MITRE Corporation)

should be driven by the mandate to help the user carry out his or her tasks. The key to designing a useful digital library listing lies in understanding which combination of attributes will help your audience find the resources they are looking for. The IA challenge is to discover the best layout and navigation of digital library listings that will help your users find the resources they need.

For instance, digital library assets at MITRE are found in various formats (journal, e-book, abstract, full-text), come from various sources (internal, external), and can be available through different accounts (free to the public, by subscription to MITRE, only through IS staff). Some resources require user login; others do not. Each falls under one or more subject taxonomy terms, and many have additional metadata such as user-supplied keywords. For some tasks, a user may want to find those assets that are available only through IS staff. For other tasks, it may be more important to the user to find assets that are both "good enough" and are easy to get to—those that do not require login, for example.

When designing the navigation part of the list, it is important to consider different finding habits. For instance, when looking for known items, people tend to use a previously-formed mental map and follow familiar cues ("click the digital library link, now select the Alpha listing, then scroll down near the

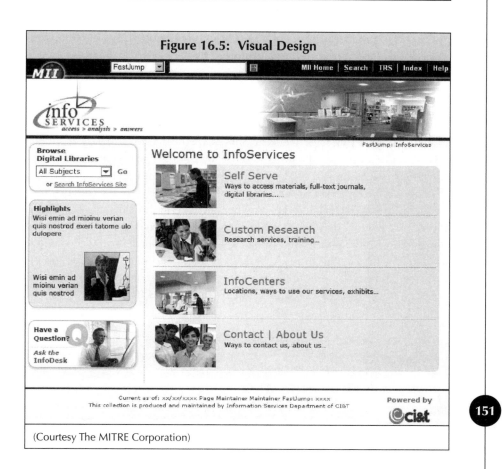

Figure 16.5: Visual Design

(Courtesy The MITRE Corporation)

top of J to find *Jane's Fighting Ships*"). However, when looking for new sources of information, people often browse, scan, and evaluate candidates and might focus on quite different cues. In this case, providing the capacity to expand and restrict result sets can be a great help, so it is important to design a search-and-browse interface that lets people interact with the field of results.

However, list navigation may be appropriate to one's technological base, bandwidth, and implementation timeframe. For instance, a hand-coded HTML page that shows works by author and another hand-coded page sorted by subject may be a great improvement over the single subject list you have now and can probably be put into place fairly quickly. Or it may be that your users really need a faceted browse that lets them scan, sort, filter, drill down, and widen the field of results by five different parameters. Or a Web 2.0 implementation that gives the user the ability to select, group, save, export, and merge information resources across a wide number of attributes and sources might be mission critical—and feasible—for your environment and your audience.

Based on internal discussions, user tests, and conversations with outside industry leaders, the team decided to offer a clean and simple interface to all available digital libraries (Figure 16.6). This page makes a clear distinction between external resources and MITRE knowledge. The team also decided to make "All Digital Libraries" the central service. Access to journal subscriptions is offered through the Serials Solutions service, but those journals are also kept in the All Digital Libraries database. Similarly, access to IT advisory services is now separated out, but the links to those services are also kept in All Digital Libraries. Users can still use familiar paths to known resources, but resource discovery is greatly aided by the addition of a new service and a new distinction.

Internal MITRE catalogs are not yet integrated with digital libraries, but in future phases they may be combined. Category and navigation taxonomies, integrated with the various internal catalogs, would make decentralized content available in the digital libraries results list pages and could also allow these assets to show up in an enterprise-wide search along with the appropriate context (e.g., "brought to you by Information Services").

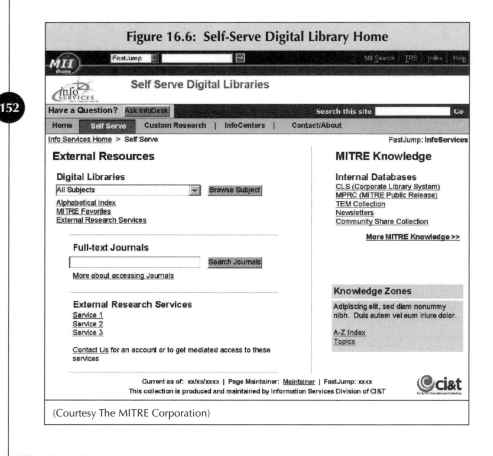

Figure 16.6: Self-Serve Digital Library Home

(Courtesy The MITRE Corporation)

The team is considering two different approaches to Digital Libraries results pages: A simple choice of views and a faceted browse navigation. Based on the results of further user testing, the team may implement a simple version in the near future and develop the faceted browse in the next phase of the project. The simple version offers the three list views available on the current site (Subject, Alpha, Favorites) while incorporating some improvements in layout, navigation, and cueing through icons (Figure 16.7).

The faceted browse version, on the other hand, lets the user narrow and widen results sets along several facets (Figure 16.8). For instance, a user could drill down to aviation-related journals available only by subscription.

When the Goal Lies Outside the Digital Library

When browsing in a digital library, the work you ultimately wish to reach— the target object—might reside anywhere. It may be in the current collection, somewhere else on the corporate intranet, or it could be behind the login page

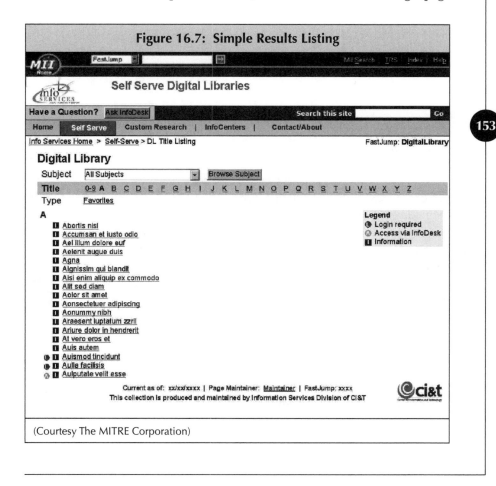

Figure 16.7: Simple Results Listing

(Courtesy The MITRE Corporation)

153

Figure 16.8: Faceted Browse

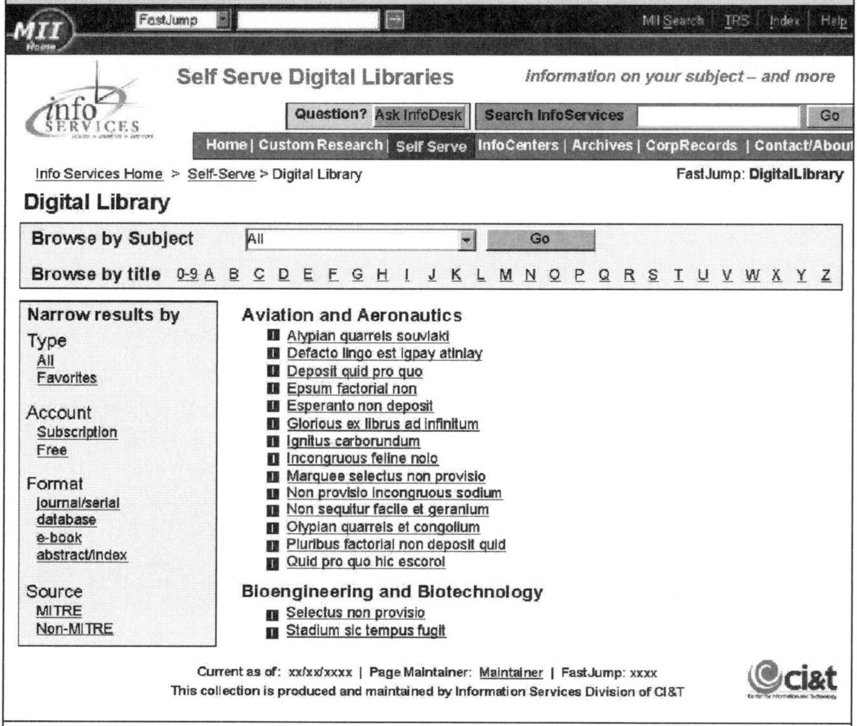

(Courtesy The MITRE Corporation)

of a service to which your digital library subscribes. The link you see in the listing might go to the thing itself or it might be a jump-off page for yet another digital library with its own navigation scheme and style of listing.

Several questions arise out of a user-centered design approach. How do we design the user experience to include smooth transitions between the digital library home page, a filtered list of results, and the new interface that may arise when clicking through? Should we—or can we—bring target objects into our own digital library sphere? Can we subsume subscription login under the corporate or library login? Or must users be on their own once they reach for certain sorts of information objects? And if they must, how do we ease the path for them? At some future point, Service Oriented Architectures (SOAs), which are built of loosely coupled, interoperable components and link content across distributed repositories, should greatly facilitate the creation of smooth, enterprise-wide knowledge systems. But until SOAs are widely in place, serious workarounds will be needed. And each design team must make considered decisions on how best to smooth the way for their users.

In phase II of the project, the team was concentrating on improving navigation and consistency in the internal IS collection itself and was deferring tackling the larger issue of achieving a unified user experience across external information spaces. In phase III, the team will weigh the merits and feasibility of a number of approaches, including importing external records into the centralized Digital Libraries database, adding contextual help around certain information objects that clarifies how to handle them (e.g., logging in and searching external databases), and adding external interface types to the list of facets users can browse in order to set user expectations about what they will encounter when they click through to various sorts of external databases.

Conclusion

Web sites are becoming more responsive to individuals and communities. Well-behaved sites react to users' actions in natural ways. They anticipate needs in a nonintrusive manner, play nicely with other Web and non-Web tools, let users interact by adding and tagging content and working collaboratively in groups, and do not force users to bend themselves into awkward shapes to work within a site's design. People are coming to expect Web sites to be shaped to fit *them*, and digital libraries need to live up to this promise.

Fortunately, with information architecture methodologies, a user-centered design approach, and sensible project management, you have the tools to build fully articulated frameworks for all kinds of Web creations. All that remains to animate your site is the spark of your inspiration—and the participation of your users.

155

Chapter 17

Usability Case Study: NASA Goddard Library

Andrea Japzon
and Kathleen McGlaughlin

Context

The Goddard Space Flight Center has two libraries, the Homer E. Newell Memorial Library in Greenbelt, Maryland, and the Wallops Flight Facility Technical Library in Wallops Island, Virginia. The Greenbelt Library supports more than 7,200 civil servant and contractor employees, while the Wallops Library serves 800. The libraries' users are primarily scientists and engineers. Administrators and project managers are the next largest group of library users. Of the 10 NASA Centers, Goddard has the largest research staff with approximately 6,000 scientists and engineers. The library supports the work performed at Goddard, which primarily is designing, building, and deploying research instruments and satellites in Earth's orbit and in space. The Hubble Space Telescope and Landsat are two of Goddard's longstanding and well-known projects.

Engineering, earth science, astronomy, space science, mathematics, computer science, physics, management, aerospace, and chemistry are the subject areas of focus for the Goddard Libraries. The most frequently used electronic resources include ISI's Web of Knowledge, IEEE Xplore, and INSPEC. Both libraries are staffed with reference librarians, and e-mail reference service is supported. The library's staff is composed of government contractors and civil servants who work together as a team to provide library services to their customers. Use of the physical library has decreased as the availability of digital resources has increased. Virtual or desktop access to the Goddard Library has become the norm, with 25,000 users a month visiting the library's Web site, also known as the Goddard Digital Library.

From 1998 to 2005, the library's Web site grew as new digital resources were acquired. The initial architecture was primarily designed to provide

157

information about library resources and services and links to a few online resources. The underlying infrastructure did not change over the years as the content changed. Resources were added when and where they made the most sense. The site's primary means of navigation, which consisted of four center image buttons, each linking to a separate section of the Web site, was completely overlooked by many users. As a result, the "Quick Picks" menu on the right side of the screen, which represented only a selection of the resources available in the site, was used almost exclusively for navigation (Figure 17.1).

The Challenge

In 2005, the NASA Goddard Space Flight Center Library was mandated to bring its Web site into conformity with new NASA-wide Web templates, part of the One NASA initiative being implemented with the goal of creating efficiencies in operations across all NASA centers. One area addressed by this initiative was Web site design: One NASA promoted the use of a common "look and feel" for every NASA Web site.

The primary challenge in using the new One NASA templates would be developing a unique Web identity for the library. The culture of each NASA

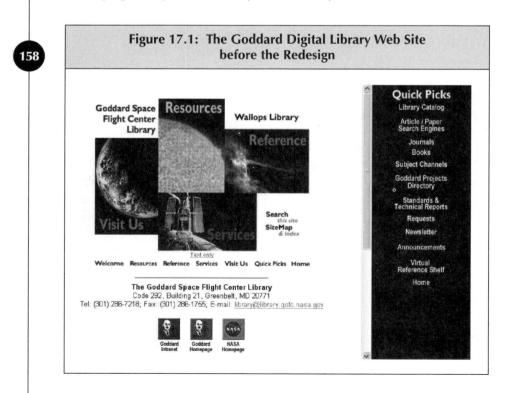

Figure 17.1: The Goddard Digital Library Web Site before the Redesign

Center is unique, and some Goddard employees had expressed resistance to the idea that the new One NASA policy could satisfy the unique needs of every Web site at every center. The need to incorporate the new One NASA templates, in addition to the fact that the site was never subjected to user testing, led the library's Web team leader and the information scientist to decide it was time to perform usability testing on the Goddard Library Web site.

When developing the plan for the library Web site usability testing project, the authors of this chapter presented a case to the library director, who is a civil servant, for consideration. She was very enthusiastic about the plan and approved it immediately. Support from upper management in any institution is of vital importance to any redesign, as they can provide resources and political support—both essential to the success of a major redesign project.

Process

The usability study was developed using an iterative design process and was influenced by Jakob Nielsen's general philosophy of Web testing. The methodology utilized in-house staff expertise combined with an innovative use of the library's existing technology for capturing and digitizing Webcasts to produce Web analysis sessions. The sessions captured comments from the testers and the onscreen paths they followed during their testing sessions. The sessions were reviewed in depth, analyzed, and compiled into a usability report that set a clear path for the redesign.

Roles assigned to staff during the testing and Web redesign project were based on individual skills, not employment status. The cross-disciplinary team consisted of 10 members with varying degrees of responsibility and involvement. The roles included a project leader, Web page designers and editors, an audiovisual technician, usability testers, test reviewers, and report writers. Both librarians and non-librarians participated on the team to provide the widest possible perspective on the feedback received from the library's customers.

The technique of asking participants questions and having them think aloud was used for the testing process. Ten online library tasks were read aloud to participants, who were also provided a print copy of the questions. Followup questions were used to stimulate the participants to think aloud as they worked through the tasks and at the completion of each one. The tasks were designed to identify issues with design, layout, copy, or technical structure throughout the entire site. Appendix 17A illustrates the approach to interacting with the usability participants.

As part of their training and in order to increase the team members' comfort level with administering the usability test, the team first held practice sessions with staff members as participants. Additionally, the first test participants were individuals who were known to be friendly, making the first real session easier to administer. One question was changed after the first test, as it turned out to be almost impossible to answer given the state of the site design.

Three members of the Web site redesign team were trained by the authors to administer the test instrument to a total of 10 participants. Participants were selected to represent a diversity of ages, positions held, and gender. For persons of high social position—for example, the Chief Information Officer—a letter was sent requesting their participation in the testing. Other participants were recruited simply by approaching them in the library or cafeteria and asking them for their participation. These strategies worked, as the testing participants were both diverse and extremely interested in helping the library.

One of the three trained team members met with each participant individually in an office in the library designated for the testing. The sessions, which followed the script as detailed in Appendix 17A, lasted approximately one hour. At the close of each session, a single Windows Media file was saved that preserved the entire session, including the audio and onscreen activities.

Equipment

The team used the library's existing technological capabilities for capturing and digitizing Webcasts of on-Center presentations to record and produce the Web analysis sessions. The equipment included a computer, Windows Media Encoder, and a microphone. Windows Media Encoder is a tool for content producers who want to capture audio and video content. Other screen capture software products, such as SnagIt or Camtasia, which also capture the participant's mouse movements, clicks, and typed responses, were considered. However, using the Windows Media Encoder along with a microphone allowed for the simultaneous capture of the testers' onscreen activity synchronized with their spoken comments and responses during the test.

Analysis

Each session file was reviewed in depth by two different team members who were not involved in administering the particular test under review; two team members working separately provided a broader analytical perspective than just one. Thus, if two different reviewers identified the same issues within a session, the resulting recommendation for a change was stronger. In this way, the two reviewers provided both a thorough analysis and a check against the other's findings.

The authors developed an analysis guide to provide consistency. Each reviewer was given a copy of the guide, which included a list of questions to assist with their analysis. For example, on task eight, "Please find a list of resources created by a librarian on Chaos or Concurrent Engineering," the reviewers were given the following questions to help them:

- Was the "Reference" button the obvious choice?
- Did this term make sense to the participant for obtaining a bibliography?
- Did Subject Channels or Subject Guides make sense to them?
- Was another term suggested?
- Is this type of information of value to them?
- Did they indicate if they would use it again?

The reviewers were encouraged to make comments outside of the guide, but all reviewers found that the guide was very helpful to them in their analysis.

The reviewers submitted their analyses as a series of reports, which were then synthesized by the authors and compiled into a final usability report that set a clear path for the subsequent redesign project. The report was presented to the library director who approved it and encouraged the Web Team to move forward with all the redesign recommendations outlined in the report.

Findings

Too Many Searches!

Almost everything on the library's Web site involves some type of search. There is a site search, a federated search, a multitude of subscription databases, locally developed databases, and more. During testing, the usability participants were confused by the functionality of the different searches and were not always sure which search was appropriate for the tasks presented. From this, the team learned that they needed to guide users in selecting the best search mechanism possible.

The Web team took this feedback and worked with the library's customers to simplify the search functions in the final design of the Web site. All the library Web site searches were consolidated into one section, aptly called "Search." In that section, patrons could select the sort of searching they wanted to do by organizing the searches by type (journal article, eBook, technical report, etc.) and by subject (earth science, astronomy, physics, etc.) This provided users with a narrowed set of possible resources to search. These lists also included information about each of the resources to further assist the patron with deciding on the best tool to use. The various searches were also listed alphabetically to aid the patron who knew exactly what they wanted to search (i.e., Web of Science). Finally, the most popular search resources, as identified by the patrons, were provided directly on the front page. Included in that set was a federated search tool, which simultaneously searches 50 of the library's most popular resources.

During testing, participants also made it very clear that certain subscription databases and the library's catalog were used more frequently than other resources, and they wanted immediate access to them. To many patrons, it was as if accessing the Goddard Library Web site only equated to accessing ISI's Web of Knowledge or the library catalog. As a result, the Web team incorporated what would be the primary content of the databases or electronic resources page for most library Web sites into the main space of the library's main index page. This included links directly to the library's most popular online resources. The library's programmer even coded search boxes to the most heavily used resources directly into this main page for quick no-click search results directly from the main page of the site.

The Navigation Needs Help

During testing, participants did not notice or use the side navigation bar that was a key element of the One NASA template design. The participants said repeatedly throughout the testing that they thought supplemental drop-down menus would be the best solution. The Web Team responded by developing additional drop-down navigation menus for the top navigation buttons, while leaving the side navigation intact. The drop-down menus, which include links to each page or section under that button, were tested and found to be Section 508(b) compliant by the Goddard accessibility coordinator. They were accessible to all individuals independent of the devices used and therefore supported interaction with assistive technology. This top navigation bar was included in every page of the site, which also improved the overall navigation of the site for everyone. Now, almost every page on the site can be accessed from any other page within one or two clicks (Figure 17.2).

The Web Team also changed the navigation content and text based on the usability feedback. The three main buttons on the top navigation bar now reflect the three main types of information sought by users: Library information, search, and project information. Additionally, "Home" and "Wallops Library" links were included as top navigational buttons. The term "search" was used instead of "databases" or "electronic resources" because to the participants and many of the users in the Goddard community, the term "database" refers to something containing scientific or numerical data rather than citations or articles.

The library information section includes all information pertaining to the library, including hours, library card applications, news, and so forth. The search provides consolidated access to all aspects of searching available on the library Web site, including a federated search, the library catalog, a journals title search, information about finding technical reports and standards, an images database, an Ask A Librarian link, and more. The project information button links to a section of the site where all aspects of information related to Goddard projects were consolidated. Every new project to design and build a satellite or complete a mission at Goddard generates hundreds to thousands of

Figure 17.2: Top Navigation Bar

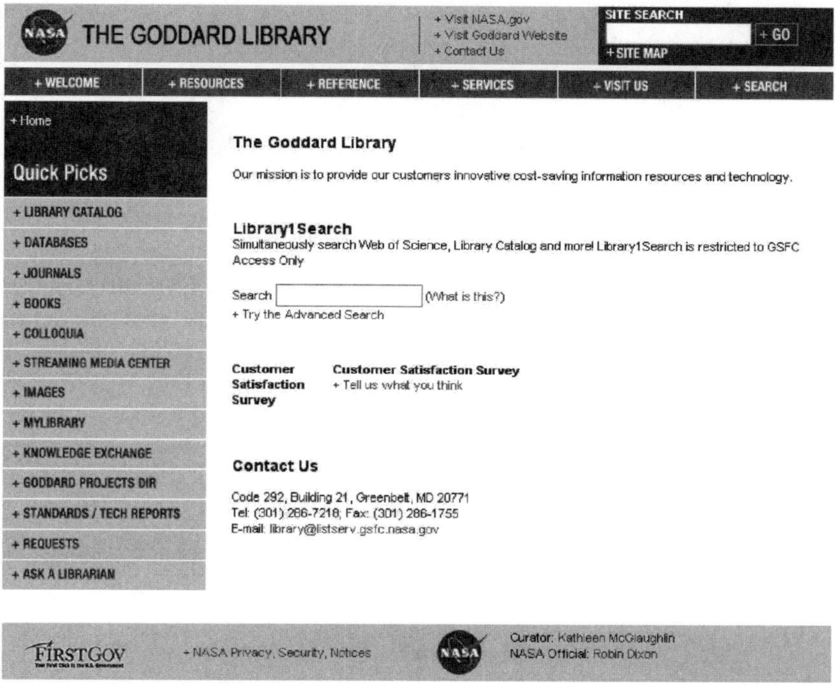

NASA — THE GODDARD LIBRARY

+ Visit NASA.gov
+ Visit Goddard Website
+ Contact Us

SITE SEARCH + GO
+ SITE MAP

+ WELCOME   + RESOURCES   + REFERENCE   + SERVICES   + VISIT US   + SEARCH

+ Home

Quick Picks

+ LIBRARY CATALOG
+ DATABASES
+ JOURNALS
+ BOOKS
+ COLLOQUIA
+ STREAMING MEDIA CENTER
+ IMAGES
+ MYLIBRARY
+ KNOWLEDGE EXCHANGE
+ GODDARD PROJECTS DIR
+ STANDARDS / TECH REPORTS
+ REQUESTS
+ ASK A LIBRARIAN

The Goddard Library

Our mission is to provide our customers innovative cost-saving information resources and technology.

Library1Search
Simultaneously search Web of Science, Library Catalog and more! Library1Search is restricted to GSFC Access Only

Search [   ]   (What is this?)
+ Try the Advanced Search

Customer Satisfaction Survey
Customer Satisfaction Survey   + Tell us what you think

Contact Us

Code 292, Building 21, Greenbelt, MD 20771
Tel: (301) 286-7218; Fax: (301) 286-1755
E-mail: library@listserv.gsfc.nasa.gov

FIRSTGOV   + NASA Privacy, Security, Notices

Curator: Kathleen McGlaughlin
NASA Official: Robin Dixon

163

technical documents, plans, drawings, design reviews, modification, and test results. This type of information, along with the human resources assigned to each project, constitutes project information. The team found during testing that Goddard scientists and engineers are particularly interested in this specific information.

Eliminate Librarian Language

During testing, it was found that the word 'reference' was meaningless to the usability participants. It was also found that the bibliographies carefully created for users were perceived to be of no value. Comments such as the following about the bibliographies were difficult but important to hear: "They are a shot in the dark—you don't know what topics will be covered or from what perspective"; "What could a librarian possibly know about chaos theory that I don't already know"; "Google is the 21st-century bibliography maker." As a result, the Web team no longer creates topical bibliographies for the library's users. Now librarians can spend more time creating online tutorials and promoting the library's resources through outreach activities.

"Everyone Else is Doing It!":
Employ Universal Web Functionality

The team learned from participants that it is important to employ universally expected Web functionality when possible. FAQs were looked for (but not found) by most of the participants and were requested. Thus a "How do I . . . ?" drop down menu was added to the top right section of the main page. This presentation of frequently asked questions is widely used by other libraries and therefore is easily recognizable. Likewise, many libraries use the phrase "Ask a Librarian" to indicate to users where they can go to ask a question online or gain access to a librarian. All the participants knew the purpose of Ask a Librarian and thought favorably of this service. The team made Ask a Librarian available on every page of the site. Participants expected to find the site search in the top right-hand corner of a Web site. The Web team took advantage of this knowledge by incorporating site search into the site in a way that is expected by the library's patrons.

Meeting the Needs of Users

Four Generations

The Goddard Library's users span four generations and form two distinct user groups. The four generations employed at Goddard are—starting with the oldest—the Veterans (1925 to 1945), the Baby Boomers (1946 to 1964) and Generations X (1965 to 1980) and Y (1981 to 2001). The team's interest in understanding these generations stems from the noticeable difference in technology adoption amongst them. Goddard employees and the general public are the two distinct user groups, both of whom have very different information needs. Some unexpected responses came from the usability testing regarding these different groups and generations.

The younger generation wanted a more dynamic site with greater interactivity, and asked the library to add RSS news feeds and linking from Google Scholar. The team has since incorporated these features. During the usability testing sessions, participants expressed no great interest in the resources presented via the virtual reference shelf, which included links to freely available reference sites and to a variety of search engines. As a result, the team did not include the reference shelf in the site redesign. However, almost immediately, the library began receiving phone calls from the Veteran generation asking what happened to it. Since then, the virtual reference shelf has been revised and returned to the library's site. Most people at Goddard loved the changes to the site, but the library did receive some complaints. A few individuals, who fell into the Baby Boomer or Veteran categories, could not find certain resources because they were disoriented by the new design.

In response to their calls, the team explained the benefits of the new design and invited them in for a personal meeting regarding their recommendations for the site. The team found that, by working with the patrons who complained, they were able to turn the situation into a positive one. By the end of most of these discussions, the formerly unhappy patrons had bought into the new site enthusiastically.

Internal and External Users

Part of NASA's mission is to inspire the next generation through public outreach. The library supports this mission through its Web site by making the catalog publicly available, answering public reference questions, and providing access to NASA/Goddard resources in the public domain. Prior to the redesign, the library maintained only one Web site and blocked unauthorized access to subscription resources. An icon next to a resource in the old site indicated that it was for Goddard Center employees only. During the usability process, the team focused on the library's primary user population, Goddard's researchers and scientists. This forced the team to revisit the feasibility of meeting the needs of two audiences with one Web site. Not only were their levels of interest different, but providing unfettered access to resources for both audiences was becoming increasingly difficult, particularly as Goddard continued to extend its digital library. After much discussion, the team concluded that providing two sites—one developed specifically for the public and one for the Goddard community—was the best answer. Re-examining the library's mission statement clarified the need to focus efforts on the primary audience: The Goddard community. This decision resulted in two sites: A public Extranet site consisting of nine pages containing the best of the best public information related to Goddard's mission, and a "Center" site comprising several hundred pages and multiple tools, services, and resources. The new public site continues the library's outreach goal, but does not require much maintenance. The staff now focuses energy on bringing the best possible resources and tools to the primary community the library exists to serve.

Conclusion

The Web Site Redesign

The Web team has proceeded with the Web site redesign and in the process trimmed the site from thousands of pages to a few hundred. The new Web interface provides access to a wealth of information resources and services, including such customer-requested items as drop-down navigation menus and a "How do I ... ?" feature that guides new customers to the most frequently used resources and services. The library responded to customer feedback by consolidating and reorganizing the highly sought-after Goddard project information by making it a prominent feature on the Web site. The team also added a new, dynamically generated news section, complete with RSS feeds to the main page (Figure 17.3). All the library's resources were restructured for a streamlined site that is comprehensive, yet easy to use.

This new multifaceted Web site successfully meets the library's goal of meeting the internal needs of Goddard's scientists and engineers, while externally accomplishing NASA's mission of providing the public with information.

The new Web site was launched at the library's annual open-house event and promoted through the library's newsletter and Goddard's local newspaper of record, *Goddard News*. Feedback on the new site was solicited at all venues and via the Web site itself.

Award-Winning Process

In April 2006, the library's Web team was awarded a Goddard Award of Excellence for developing this usability process that supported the library's Web site redesign. The library was one of the first units at Goddard to use usability testing as the basis for Web site design. A staff member from the Office of Public Affairs charged with redesigning her department's Web site heard about the library's usability testing and contacted the team for help. The team assisted her with developing the questions for the study, provided training on

166

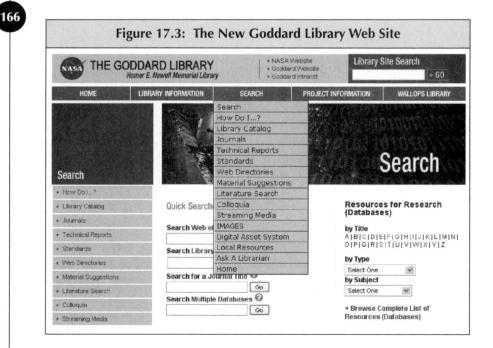

Figure 17.3: The New Goddard Library Web Site

the process, and provided her with library equipment to test her site. Further, in an effort to continue promoting user-centered Web design, the library has created a test lab in the library to facilitate usability testing at the Center, and have additionally shared this process with others.

While the formal recognition of the award is a prized experience, the overwhelmingly positive feedback from library users has been the most important recognition of the Web team's effort to create a user-centered design. Through both the inclusion of library's users in the Web site redesign and the promotion of their inclusion in the process, the Web team was able to create a connection with the users of the Goddard Digital Library and reinforce the library's role as a vital institution within Goddard.

Appendix 17A: Usability Test Guide	
Introduction	We are planning to redesign the library's Web site, and we would like to know what is working, and what's not working. So the objective of this meeting is for me to gather information from you about how well the Web site works. I'm going to ask you to complete a series of tasks using the library Web page. Along the way, I'm going to ask you a lot of questions about the choices you make. Don't worry, I am not going to be judging your answers to my questions. Rather, I'll use your answers to judge the library Web site. Does that make sense? Do you have any questions? Along the way, be sure to give me any feedback you have about the library Web site.
Leading Questions	These were prompting questions to be used while the testers worked through each individual question. • What page would you use to answer this question? • Look at all of the different links on this page. Which is the most likely one to help you find this information? • Can you give me a reason why you decided to click on that link instead of another link on that page? • What makes "X" a more likely place than "Y"? • Take your time and think about which category would be the best choice to go to for finding the answer to this question. • Would you like to back up and start again?
Follow Up Questions	• Would you use this page more often now that you know that it is here? • Did you understand the terminology used? • What do you think the purpose of this page is? • Describe the types of resources you would expect to find on this page. • What might have helped you find this information more easily? • How would you change this page to make it clearer or easier to use?
Tasks	This is the series of online tasks we asked the test participants to complete: 1. Where on the library's Web site can borrowers find what the loan period is for books? 2. If you could not find what you were looking for on the library's Web site using the links provided, what would be your next step?
	(Cont'd.)

168

Appendix 17A: Usability Test Guide *(Continued)*

Tasks *(Cont'd.)*	3. How do you find books about "remote sensing of the environment"?
	4. How do you place an interlibrary loan request?
	5. Using the library's site, please find a contact to the Goddard Photo and Movie Gallery.
	6. How would you find the following article in the journal: "A comparison of the optical constants of aligned and unaligned thin polyfluorene films" JOURNAL OF APPLIED PHYSICS 96 (9): 4735-4741 NOV 1 2004?
	7. How would you locate the following NASA Technical Report: "Performance evaluation of the Cray X1 for Scientific Applications"?
	8. Please find a list of resources created by a librarian on "Chaos" or "Concurrent Engineering."
	9. The Goddard Library subscribes to many [search] article collections on topics such as Earth Science, Physics, and Engineering. Find the page with links to those collections. What does the word 'database' mean to you?
	10. If you needed information for a new project or work assignment, where would you start your search?

Bibliography

Accessibility

Clark, Joe. 2007. *Building Accessible Websites*. New Riders Press. Available: http://joeclark.org/book/sashay/serialization/ (accessed June 14, 2007).

> The author is a journalist and accessibility consultant. Well written and engaging, the book starts at the beginning ("Why is accessibility important?"), discussing accessibility considerations for images, links, tables, multimedia, all the way to certification.

Paciello, Mike. 2000. *Web Accessibility for People with Disabilities*. Lawrence, KS: CMP.

> Written by an internationally recognized expert in the development of accessibility standards. This easy-to-understand book covers why and how to make Web sites accessible.

Card Sorting

Maurer, Donna, and Todd Warfel. 2004. "Card Sorting: A Definitive Guide." *Boxes and Arrows* (April 7). Available: www.boxesandarrows.com/view/card_sorting_a_definitive_guide (accessed March 30, 2007).

> Written by an information architect and user experience architect, this article provides detailed information on issues such as selecting content to test, number of cards to use, and preparing the cards for later coding. Includes a script for introducing the test to participants.

Robertson, James. 2001. "Information Design Using Card Sorting." *Step Two Designs: Papers & Case Studies* (February 19). Available: www.steptwo.com.au/papers/cardsorting (accessed March 30, 2007).

> Written by a usability consultant, this paper covers the what, why, and how of card sorting, including how to record, analyze, and use the results.

Focus Group Interviews

Greenbaum, Thomas L. 2005. *The Handbook for Focus Group Research*. 2nd ed. Thousand Oaks, CA: Sage.

> Greenbaum is the author of many book and articles on focus groups and market research. This book describes ways to maximize the effectiveness of focus groups, selecting moderators, and the use of technology in conducting focus group interviews.

Morgan, David L. 1993. *Successful Focus Groups: Advancing the State of the Art.* Newbury Park, CA: Sage.

> This collection of articles covers the basics of when and how to use focus group interviews, combining focus group interviews with other methods, and specific issues related to different groups and situations.

Heuristic Evaluations

Nielsen, Jakob. 2005. "Ten Usability Heuristics." Useit.com. Available: www.useit.com/papers/heuristic/heuristic_list.html (accessed March 30, 2007).

> Nielsen's frequently cited list of 10 general principles for user interface design.

Nielsen, Jakob. "How to Conduct a Heuristic Evaluation." Useit.com. Available: www.useit.com/papers/heuristic/heuristic_evaluation.html (accessed March 30, 2007).

> Discusses why several evaluators are needed, how to conduct an evaluation, and the benefits of heuristic evaluations.

Paper Prototyping

Medero, Shawn. 2007. "Paper Prototyping." *A List Apart: For People Who Make Web-sites.* (January 23). Available: http://alistapart.com/articles/paperprototyping (accessed May 26, 2007).

> The author, an interface designer at the University of Pennsylvania, argues persuasively for the benefits of paper prototyping (easier, faster, and less intimidating for test participants). The illustrations show how paper prototypes can be used to model a variety of situations (drop down menus, error conditions) and record users' actions for later study.

Snyder, Carolyn. 2003. *Paper Prototyping: The Fast and Easy Way to Design and Refine User Interfaces.* San Diego, CA: Morgan, Kaufmann.

> Written by a usability engineer and consultant, this book describes the benefits of paper prototypes (speed, ease of use, and low cost), includes a step-by-step guide to conducting usability tests with paper prototypes, and addresses the differences from testing with working interfaces. Notes pros and cons of paper prototyping and includes case studies.

Surveys

Alreck, Pamela, and Robert Settle. 2003. *The Survey Research Handbook.* 3rd ed. New York: McGraw-Hill/Irwin.

> Well written, comprehensive guide to conducting surveys that will be helpful to novice and experienced researchers alike. This book has become a standard tool in the field.

Rea, Louis M., and Richard A. Parker. 2005. *Designing and Conducting Survey Research: A Comprehensive Guide.* 3rd ed. San Francisco: Jossey-Bass.

> This is a thorough overview of survey research, and also includes detailed explanations of current techniques and analysis methods.

Schonlau, Matthias, et al. 2002. *Conducting Research Surveys via E-mail and the Web.* Santa Monica, CA: Rand.

Good overview of the issues and challenges facing researchers who wish to use electronic methods for conducting surveys. The basics are well covered and relevant today.

University of Texas at Austin. Division of Instructional Innovation and Assessment. 2007. "Survey How To" (last updated June 10). Available: www.utexas.edu/academic/diia/assessment/iar/how_to/methods/survey.php (accessed June 14, 2007).

No longer available online but at the time of this writing, this was a concise yet helpful and well-thought out overview of survey basics filled with examples of good and bad questions, and which links users to further information where appropriate.

Usability Testing

Articles

Augustine, Susan, and Courtney Greene. 2002. "Discovering How Students Search a Library Web Site: A Usability Case Study." *College & Research Libraries* 63, no. 4 (July): 354–365.

A case study from the University of Illinois–Chicago Library, the article describes the process and results of a typical usability test. Twelve undergrads were tested on 20 tasks.

Cockrell, Barbara J., and Elaine A. Jayne. 2002. "How Do I Find an Article? Insights from a Web Usability Study." *Journal of Academic Librarianship* 28, no. 3 (May): 122–133.

The authors, librarians at Western Michigan University, were involved in a usability test of the library Web site, focusing on ease of finding articles. Starts with a review of the literature and goes into detail on their findings.

Genuis, Shelagh. 2004. "Web Site Usability Testing: A Critical Tool for Libraries." *Feliciter* 50, no. 4: 161–164.

A concise overview of library Web site usability testing, including tables of methods and a list of usability resources.

Books

Dumas, Joseph. S., and Janice C. Redish. 1999. *A Practical Guide to Usability Testing.* Rev. ed. Bristol, UK: Intellect.

This book goes beyond Web site usability testing, covering the broader areas of usability engineering and interface design, while keeping the language simple and using lots of examples.

Nielsen, Jakob. 1993. *Usability Engineering.* Boston: Academic Press.

Though this authoritative text on the subject by the preeminent usability author was written in 1993, it is still relevant and useful today.

Pearrow, Mark. 2000. *Web Site Usability Handbook.* Rockland, MA: Charles River Media.

Although directed at a corporate audience, with its focus on user-centered design and coverage of the main usability tools, this is a good guide for usability. Provides useful background information on human factors research and statistical methods.

173

Rubin, J. 1994. *Handbook of Usability Testing: How to Plan, Design, and Conduct Effective Tests*. New York: Wiley.

> This classic text uses an easy-to-follow, step-by-step format to guide new usability practitioners from concept to implementation. In simple language, Rubin describes fundamental goals and elements for four types of tests. Attention is given to test preparation for optimum results—how to construct a test, how to set up the test environment, and how the test moderator should behave.

Spool, Jared. 1999. *Web Site Usability: A Designer's Guide*. San Francisco: Morgan Kaufmann.

> Reports on usability testing of nine sites where participants were asked to find four types of information on each site.

Online Newsletters

Nielsen, Jakob. 1995–present. "Alertbox: Current Issues in Web Usability." Available: www.useit.com/alertbox/ (accessed June 14, 2007).

> Nielsen is the guru of Web usability. This bi-weekly column is essential reading for anyone involved in Web usability.

User Interface Engineering. "UIE Brain Sparks." Available: www.uie.com/brainsparks

> Brainsparks is a blog that is a "repository for everything cool and interesting that is happening in the world of designing usable Web sites and systems."

Web Site Usability (General)

Style guide

Lynch, Patrick, and Sarah Horton. 2005. *Web Style Guide*. 2nd ed. (Last updated July 12). Available: www.webstyleguide.com/ (accessed June 14, 2007).

> The guide is comprehensive and thorough in its coverage of all aspects of Web site design. The entire book is available online in an easy-to-use format.

Terminology

Kupersmith, John. 2007. *Library Terms That Users Understand*. Available: www.jkup. net/terms.html (accessed June 14, 2007).

> Kupersmith has become an authority on jargon-free Web sites, giving many workshops and lectures on the topic. This site is very useful for quickly checking questionable terms, exploring best practices, and finding data and more information on terminology pitfalls and troubleshooting.

Web sites

Horton, Sarah. 2006. *Universal Usability: A Universal Design Approach to Web Usability*. Available: http://universalusability.com (accessed June 14, 2007).

> The Universal Usability site houses an unabridged, online version of *Access by Design: A Guide to Universal Usability for Web Designers*, by Sarah Horton, published in 2005 by New Riders Press.

OCLC. 2007. *OCLC Human-Computer Interaction*. Available: www.oclc.org/policies/usability/default.htm (accessed June 14, 2007).

This Web site includes a variety of instructional materials for task-based tests and heuristic tests. It reviews the basic rules of usability and shows how one reputable organization puts it to practice.

U.S. Department of Health & Human Services. "Usability.gov: Your Guide for Developing Usable and Useful Web Sites." Available: www.usability.gov (accessed June 14, 2007).

This is a large, well-developed site that covers all the usability basics. There is an emphasis on government Web sites, but the information provided is widely applicable.

Usability Professionals' Association. Available: www.upassoc.org (accessed June 14, 2007).

The Usability Professionals' Association's Web site is an excellent resource for information on all aspects of usability, including Web design, and has many links of interest to those who want to understand the field in depth.

Web Server Log Analysis

Jansen, Bernard J. 2006. "Search Log Analysis: What It Is, What's Been Done, How to Do It." *Library & Information Science Research* 28, no. 3 (Autumn): 407–432.

This is an extensive and thorough examination of the state-of-the-art but often overlooked analysis tool. The methodology presented ensures that maximum value is obtained from Web server logs.

175

About the Editors and Contributors

The Editors

Tom Lehman is Digital Access Librarian at the University Libraries of Notre Dame, where he chairs teams that help maintain metadata in the library Web site, carry out usability assessments of the library Web site, and oversee the library intranet. He also participates in the maintenance of the university search engine. Prior to his current position, he was head of Copy Cataloging. In his spare time he digitizes 35mm slides taken in Puerto Rico in the 1940s and 1950s, preserving and providing access to them.

Terry Nikkel is Director, Information Services and Systems, at the Saint John campus of the University of New Brunswick. Previously, he was Head, Library Systems, at Dalhousie University in Halifax, Nova Scotia. Terry has been involved in many Web site projects and has long had a keen interest in interface usability and design. Terry was recently appointed to a university-wide steering committee at UNB that will oversee a complete overhaul of all its external and internal Web sites. Terry earned his MLIS at the University of Western Ontario, and recently completed an MBA at Dalhousie.

The Contributors

Alison Aldrich is a health sciences reference librarian at Wright State University. She also serves on the Libraries' Web team. Alison has a Master of Science in Information degree from the University of Michigan and a Master of Public Health degree from Wright State University.

Vishwam Annam works as a senior programmer/Web developer at Wright State University Libraries. He has been involved in programming, researching, and teaching in academic libraries for more than six years. He received a Master of Science degree in Computer Science from Western Kentucky University. Vishwam is interested in investigating the way library users interact with information technology, both how they affect technological development and how they are affected by technology.

Martin Courtois is coordinator of the institutional repository at Kansas State University. Over the past 30 years, Courtois has worked as a reference and instruction librarian at several academic institutions, and since 2000 has been involved in designing and conducting Web usability tests.

Michelle Dalmau is the digital projects and usability librarian for the Indiana University Digital Library Program (DLP), where she is responsible for coordinating and managing digital library projects, as well as coordinating and leading user studies for the DLP and the greater Indiana University Bloomington Libraries. Her research interests include the integration of complex metadata structures with discovery functionality of digital resources, as well as pedagogic use of digital resources.

Nora Dimmock is the head of the Multimedia Center at the University of Rochester's Rush Rhees Library and the subject specialist for Film and Media Studies. She is an active member of the library's Web site usability team and the College Diversity Roundtable. Her research interests include usability, digital copyright issues, and popular culture collections in academic libraries.

Juliet L. Hardesty is a systems analyst/programmer at Indiana University. Currently, her duties include programming for the university's online library catalog and the library Web site on the main Bloomington campus. She is also involved in usability testing on both systems and is a member of the Usability Working Group at Indiana University.

Andrea Japzon is currently a PhD student at the College of Information Science & Technology at Drexel University. She is supported by an IMLS fellowship. Her research interests include information behaviors, personal information management, digital preservation, and information literacy. She has worked as a librarian for the New York Public Library, the Hunter College Library, the Enoch Pratt Free Library, and the NASA Goddard Space Flight Center Library.

Megan Johnson is the Web services librarian at Belk Library and Information Commons, Appalachian State Library in Boone, NC. Her research interests include usability testing of library related interfaces.

Leslie Johnston is the head of Digital Access Services at the University of Virginia Library, where she manages digital library program components supporting the collection, management, and delivery of digital content. Previously, she served as the head of Instructional Technology and Library Information

Systems at the Harvard Design School, as the academic technology specialist for Art for the Stanford University Libraries, and as database specialist for the Getty Research Institute. Ms. Johnston has also been active in the museum automation community, working for various museums, teaching courses on museum systems, editing the journal *Spectra*, and serving on the board of the Museum Computer Network.

Hal P. Kirkwood, Jr. is the associate head at the Management & Economics Library of Purdue University. He is responsible for coordinating instruction activities and Web site design. His research interests include alternative methods of teaching business information literacy, Web site usability testing, and concept mapping. He is currently chair of the Business & Finance Division of the Special Libraries Association.

Shelley McKibbon is an information services librarian at Dalhousie University in Halifax, Nova Scotia. She works primarily with schools in the Faculty of Health professions, and is also responsible for training in bibliographic management software packages.

Kathleen McGlaughlin has worked at the NASA Goddard Space Flight Center Library since 1995 as the library's Web site developer. Three years ago, she took on the additional role of systems team leader, and in January 2007, she became the deputy program manager for the library. Throughout, she has been involved in every aspect of building the Goddard Digital Library as it exists today, and was the co-lead in implementing the Goddard Library Web site usability study and subsequent redesign, a project for which the Library's Web Team won a Goddard Award of Excellence.

Julianne Morian currently serves as the head of Electronic Services at the Clinton-Macomb Public Library in Michigan. She holds a graduate degree from the University of Michigan in Human-Computer Interaction. Before entering the librarianship field, she worked as a usability specialist for a Web design firm in Ann Arbor, MI.

Brenda Reeb coordinates the usability program at the University of Rochester in Rochester, New York. Her interests include user-centered design, business information, and government information.

Stacy Surla's diverse interests—science, literature, performance art—led her from multimedia to the Web to information architecture as a user-centered field of practice. She still cultivates an eclectic set of fascinations, including building communities of practice and reading Victorian novels. An IA at the MITRE Corporation, Ms. Surla has an MA in Literature, serves on the Board of the IA Institute, and is associate editor for the ASIS&T Bulletin.

179

Michael Yunkin is the Web content manager at the University of Nevada, Las Vegas Libraries, where he is responsible for creating and maintaining Web content, and for assisting in the implementation of various new technologies. His research interests include digital asset management and human-computer interaction.

Index

181

183